M000030829

Disclaimer: This is a non-fiction book of healing. The people and situations in this book are real, and they are not trained writers, but brothers and sisters who've experienced a loss. All stories have been formatted, but their raw content is what makes them real and true, and completely from the heart of those that wrote them.

The Last Time I Saw You is a collaboration of stories from Danielle Lee Zwissler, and her friends from The Sounds of Siblings group on Facebook.

ISBN: 9781717919991

© Copyright with Firefly & Wisp Books 2018

First Publishing June 11, 2018

Cover Art by Z Productions

FIREFLY & WISP
B O O K S

Two years ago, my brother passed away and his absence has left an empty hole in me.

The aching grief that I've experienced has been so hard to bear. I looked for people that could relate to me and my situation, I searched for books about siblings, I joined different groups, and I reached out to local grief counseling sites, and support groups. But it just seemed that there was a general lack of sympathy for the mourning siblings.

As a writer, I wanted to change that, so I spoke to those that I've met in groups, and that have had such loss, and collected their stories within these pages. Through writing support, and love, we came together to remember our lost brothers and sisters in *The Last Time I Saw You.*

If you, too, are a sibling, and you have experienced this pain, feel free to find our group online at: The Last Time I Saw You Anthology, or any of the Siblings groups on Facebook.

Remember, you're not alone.

For

Brent

Don

Judy

Kylie

Tyler

Kate

Justin

Dennis

Mary Ann

Leon

Ryan Robert

Emily

John Paul German

Jimmy Kim

Sam Shelton

Scott

Kevin

Sully

Petra

Chris

Michael

Jillian

Barry

Dave

Megan

Darren

Erin

Savanna

Keven

Diane

Adrian

Amanda

Jake

Rick

Kevin

Sara

Dee

Eric

Robby

Nicholas

David

Adam

Bobby

Danielle

Erin

Lou

Katie

Rickey

Brian

Darren

Reed

Bethany

Lindsey

Kristin

"Grief is like the ocean;

It comes on waves ebbing and flowing.

Sometimes the water is calm,

And sometimes it is overwhelming.

All we can do is learn to swim."

-Vicki Harrison

Brent Wesley Haver
September 1, 1976 – July 11, 2016

*This picture is of me (Danielle), our Dad, Wesley, my brother, Brent, and our Mom, Rise'. It's one of my favorite pictures of all of us. *

The Last Time I Saw You was when you died.

$\mathscr{L}$et me back up a little. My brother was two years older than me. We'd grown up happy, and as most siblings, we liked to pick on one another. I have a lot of great memories of Brent. We had a lot of fun together, from playing video games, to watching *Batman the Animated Series*, to swimming in our parents' pool, and going on vacations.

9

We had a great childhood.

Brent was into sports, guns, zombies, and *Batman. Anything Batman.*

I remember a lot of my brother. I remember his funny laugh, the way he teased me about things, the way his smile curved up and his hugs.

He gave great hugs.

I remember watching TV with him, arguing over the super hero shows and their transition from comic book to the big screen. I remember him sleeping on all of our vacations, getting a horrible sunburn in Hawaii, and him playing football.

He was great at everything he did.

He was an artist, a wonderful son, a great brother, an amazing husband, and a great Dad.

He had two fantastic little girls, and he was a great father to them. I imagine him now, sitting up in heaven, looking down on us and smiling. I miss him so much. We all do.

On the morning of July 7th, my brother went into the hospital. On July 11th, God brought him home. I, along with our Mom and Dad, held his hand, and watched as he took his last breath. I'm glad I was there with him. It was the most profound moment of my life. I will never forget the days, hours and minutes that led up to that moment. I will never be the same. My brother was one-of-a-kind.

I love you so much, Brent.

Love,

Your Sister,

Danielle

My brother, Don

𝒯o my brother Don who left us on May 6, 2017

The last time I saw you, my dear brother, you were lying very still on the floor, your head turned in my direction, and your eyes closed shut.

I rushed to your side; you were so cold. I tried to warm you but couldn't. I tried to wake you but knew in my heart I could not. I called your name, hoping that the sound of my voice would somehow bring you back to me, but it didn't. So, I sat beside you, and as the tears rolled down my face, I told you how very much I loved you.

Since that dark day, my life hasn't been the same. Everything changed immediately when you drew your last breath. When I remember the good times we had together, I can still see your smile.

I remember the very last smile you gave me.

If only I knew then what I know now, I would hold you so close and make sure that smile never went away.

I love you, Don.

Catherine Ashton

Carole Weigel and her sister, Judy Smith

$\mathcal{M}$y sister, Judy, was born on September 22, 1936—my parents' first child. I came along 9 years later, then my brother and younger sister. Judy was always the best "big sister" anyone could ever ask for. For as long as I can remember, she was there—always very caring and motherly to my brother, sister and me.

When I was 11, in July of 1956, Judy was away for several weeks. My mom said she was visiting our uncle and aunt near Glens Falls, New York. After returning in the spring, she decided to leave her secretarial job in the city and become a flight attendant. Her leaving home was very traumatic for my younger sister and me, as we really adored Judy and missed her so much. She later married a pilot and had a daughter in 1958, living in upstate New York. The best times were when she would come for an extended visit and spend time with us at our beach house on Long Island. She always loved the beach and would not wear shoes the entire summer. Any time we saw Judy was like a holiday for us.

Sometime in late 1989, she told us she had not been feeling well. Little did we know that she had colon cancer (probably for a long time), and in January of 1990, she was diagnosed at Stage 4. Our family was devastated. We got to see her twice after that in the hospital, and on April 7th, 1990, Judy died. Nothing worse had ever happened to our family. Her husband scattered her ashes on her favorite beach in Maine.

During a conversation with my mom after Judy's death, I somehow was able to coax her into telling me what happened to Judy during that summer of 1956. Mom said she promised Judy she would never divulge the secret that Judy kept for most of her life—that she had given birth to a baby boy who she had to give up for adoption. She was staying with our aunt and uncle in Glens Falls, NY until the baby was born. Mom said it haunted Judy all her life, wondering if he was looking for her. I can't remember crying so much as I did during that talk with my mom. It broke my heart to know that she felt she couldn't tell us.

My mom passed away in 1998 and my dad in 2005. In cleaning out the house after my dad's passing, I discovered that he saved just about everything, even pay stubs from the 1940's. One of the papers I found was a hospital bill from Glens Falls Hospital, dated July 9, 1956—it was the hospital bill from when Judy had the baby! I couldn't believe he had saved it. Something made me put it in my bag, and I kept it for years.

In late 2016, my brother decided to do a DNA test through ancestry.com to confirm the lineage of our family—we pretty much knew our family originally came from Europe. About a week later, he received an email message through ancestry.com from someone who said she was trying to help a friend, Dex, find his birth family and said my brother's DNA _matched_ her friend's 98%! She asked if anyone had given a baby up for adoption in July of 1956 in Glens Falls, NY.

We found our sister's "BABY" who is now a 61 year old man!

The elation this has brought us—and to him—is unbelievable. Though his mom is no longer here, he is ecstatic that he has finally found his birth family and has said that he will come to know the beauty of his mom through us. In June, we were able to meet with him and his wife; they live very near where he was born and we will see him again soon. He is the missing part of our family who has finally been found and we absolutely love him! We firmly believe Judy has somehow made this happen.

Thanks for letting me tell this story.

Carole Weigel

Glen Head, NY

The Three of Us

$\mathcal{M}$y siblings were my heroes, and it has always got to me that there are so many people in this world that have never or will never get to meet them. They will never get the chance to be inspired by them like I was and continue to be. They'll never get to love them like I do. Now, I finally have the chance to share their story, maybe not to the world, but to you lovely readers. The problem is, where to start? All of this has happened over the course of so many years, for a majority of my life. So how do I fit it all in? Truth is, I probably can't, but I hope to do my best to get their stories out there.

I am the oldest of three siblings. *The only one who was born without Cystic Fibrosis.* Honestly, I don't remember when I was first told about either of my siblings having the disease. I only remember growing up just knowing that they had one and knowing, but not believing, they would die at a young age. I know this probably affected me more than I ever really knew, but it never seemed like it did. The only thing I can think of that tells me I was more affected by it was the fact that my brother and I used to fight all the time about who would get to sleep in my sister's room. Now, I don't know the reasoning behind my brother always wanting to sleep in her room, but for me, it was to console me, so I could sleep.

I had this secret fear of my sister dying in the middle of the night, so I wanted to be there, so I could do something to help her if it were to happen. On the nights that I got to be with her instead of our brother, I would fall asleep to the sound of the oxygen machine she needed to use when she was sleeping. Then multiple times throughout the night, I would wake up to make sure she was still breathing.

My sister, Kylie.

My sister, Kylie, was not diagnosed with CF when she was born. It wasn't until she was around three that she was finally diagnosed. I think part of this was why she always seemed to be so much sicker than my brother, but I'm not a doctor. Kylie was born in April of 1993 and passed away in 2006. She was only thirteen years old. Now I'm not exaggerating when I say she was the strongest person I have ever known. You never saw her miserable or heard her complain about anything. She always put others above herself and never asked for anything in return. This girl loved with all she had, and I swear, had the most infectious laugh I have ever heard. Honestly, I could go on and on about her, but you get the picture.

Ky's childhood was filled with hospital stays, being hospitalized at home, pills, treatments, doctor visits—everything that doesn't make for a fun childhood. She missed out on so much. When she was in kindergarten she wanted to do ballet. She looked adorable and really seemed to enjoy it on top of it being good exercise for her. Eventually though, she became too sick to go and if I remember right, was hospitalized around the same time. She never got to go back to it. She also missed out on a lot of school and fun activities. Despite all these things you would never have any idea that she missed out on so much. I hate thinking about the childhood that was stolen from her by this disease, but to try to stay on the positive side. It's hard, though. I think about those people she may have never met and those lives she may have never touched had it not been for this disease.

Kylie was a fighter. She refused to give up. There were a few times when the doctors would tell us we needed to prepare ourselves for the worst; then the next thing we knew, she would snap out of it and pull through. I think this is what made her death so hard. She never seemed to lose...and then she did.

As I said, she was in and out of the hospital throughout her life, but around 2004-2005 things seemed to get worse. My mom eventually quit her job to stay home and take care of her; which meant we lost our insurance and part of our income which in turn eventually led to us moving from California to Iowa. About a month after we moved to Iowa, we were told that Kylie wouldn't make it to 2006 without a double lung transplant. It was August 2005. So, this started the demanding process of different tests and appointments to make sure she was strong enough to get the procedure. My parents chose to have the transplant done at a hospital in Minnesota, meaning we had to drive from Iowa to Minnesota for the tests which was roughly a 3-hour drive. Normally, it wouldn't have been bad, but we had to do it multiple times a week. My brother and I were in and out of school a lot because of this.

A couple weeks into December 2005, we got the call that there were lungs, so my mom and sister were flown to the hospital and my dad was left to drive my brother and me. We left at night, and we were up all morning waiting for everything to happen. Everything seemed to go great, she just had to be hooked up to a bunch of tubes for a while and things were looking up. They had frequent doctor appointments to go to after the surgery, so instead of commuting back and forth every other day my mom and sister got to stay at the Ronald McDonald house. The room was awesome, and we all had our own beds, and since it was Christmas time they even gave us presents. We were all happy because things seemed like they were going to get better for my sister and her health.

Little did we know this would be our last family Christmas.

Things went downhill fast. Kylie developed some kind of bacteria in her lungs that I don't even remember the name of. Then the next thing we knew, she was put on a ventilator. We heard those same words, "better start to prepare for the worst." This is Kylie we're talking about though, so after 41 days she pulled through. The only thing was, she had to learn how to do everything again. After so long on a ventilator, her muscles weren't strong enough anymore. She couldn't walk, couldn't really do anything for herself. She was different. She had to use tools to help build up strength in her arms and legs. She eventually was told she had diabetes, which is common with this type of stuff, and with all the medications she was on, she started to change in appearance. Her face got puffy and her hair started to fall out. My strong sister was getting weaker by the day. I started to see that everything was taking its toll on her. She loved when my mom would put curlers in her hair, and even that was taken from her. I remember one time she was getting frustrated that she couldn't get it out and she ended up pulling just a little too hard and all the hair that was wrapped around that curler just fell out.

She started getting frustrated because she couldn't really do anything on her own anymore. She even threw her walker out of anger. This was so out of character for her. I knew she was starting to give up. It literally broke my heart to see her like this, still does. Not too long later, she was back in the hospital and things weren't looking good. She was back on the ventilator.

Eventually the doctors told us that at this point, she could pass at any time. My parents decided instead of her passing away alone without anyone knowing would be worse than taking her off the machine and letting her pass surrounded by friends and family. I remember the day I was pulled out of school to go to the hospital to be with her. As soon as I heard my name being called to the office I knew something had happened. We all met at the hospital. We painted her hands and feet to put on paper as a keepsake. We each got to privately say our goodbyes. Then we all were in the room with her as she passed. The sound of the machine turning off made it physically hard to stand. Seeing the pain my parents felt on their faces. Watching her lips turn blue as she tried to take her last breaths. These are all things burned into my brain that I relive during those long sleepless nights, yet I can't remember how I got home from the hospital that night. I just couldn't believe my baby sister was gone.

Now obviously one death doesn't outweigh the other, but my brother's death hit me pretty hard. Tyler never seemed to be as sick as Kylie was. He didn't spend as much time in the hospital as she did. He seemed to get to enjoy more of his childhood than she did. So, when I heard he wasn't doing well, it came as a shock.

My brother, Tyler.

Oh man, was my brother a little shit. That boy knew how to find and push your buttons. It could have had a lot to do with the fact that we were 5 years apart, but we almost never got along. There was no doubt that we loved each other, but we also apparently loved to fight with each other, too.

This boy was a jokester. He loved to say witty, sarcastic things and make people laugh. He was always finding some kind of trouble to get into—building horribly put together contraptions that he would ride in or climb on; trying to find some crazy stunts he could do.

His friends and he would make these videos of themselves doing ridiculous things. For example, at a high school football game they stood in the men's restroom with a makeshift microphone and their camera and recorded themselves interviewing the men who walked in. I would have never been caught dead doing anything like that! Tyler also made videos on his own. In one video he makes up his own song that's dedicated to Ke$ha and his love for her. In another video, he records himself going down our stairs in a cardboard box and just wreaking havoc on his way down. He was someone who was loved by everyone he met. Those who were lucky enough to have their lives touched by him, have been impacted by his death.

This boy not only dealt with Cystic Fibrosis, but we also found out he had a brain tumor. I remember when my mom first told me about it. I was so mad. This happened after my sister had died. This tumor was in a really sensitive area, and I remember them having to operate as soon as they could to try to remove it. I just wondered if my family was ever going to get a break. This was another scary process that took a toll on our family. The tumor was removed; it was benign, and things ended up being okay, and it was just another bump on the road of life. It still sucked all the same.

I always believed my brother would live until his 20s or 30s. As I have said, he never seemed as sick as my sister. I thought things would be different with him. But that's the thing that sucks about CF. Things can change...and fast. I was told he wasn't doing well. He could get a double lung transplant like Kylie or choose to let the disease run its course. Tyler saw what Kylie went through. He saw how she got beat up all for nothing. So, I can't blame him when he decided not to go through with the transplant and just live whatever was left of his life. So, hospice was going to be getting involved because he had maybe 6 months to live. For some reason, I thought I would have at least 6 more months with him. We found this out the beginning of October. So, I thought about how we would get to spend the holidays with him one last time, but I was wrong.

Tyler got pneumonia and boom, I lost my brother.

Tyler passed the morning before Halloween at home with my parents. I have so much guilt because I wasn't there. I remember the night before I was thinking about staying home instead of where I was living at the time. I ended up leaving, and the next morning I shot out of bed and knew I needed to get home, but before I could the phone rang. It was my grandma calling to tell me what I already knew.

Tyler had passed away.

I fell to the ground. I couldn't drive myself home. I couldn't believe this was happening.

My whole world had finally shattered.

I was the only living child now.

Losing my siblings tore our family apart. Eventually, my parents split up. All the family gatherings that I always enjoyed started to become fewer and fewer until we just stopped having them. We stopped focusing on family, and just focused on our grief. Things have never been the same since.

I miss that old life. It doesn't even seem like it was real at times. So now, 6 years after my brother passed and almost 11 years after my sister passed, we're all still trying to figure out our lives. We have our good days and our bad days and our days where we're just consumed by the grief, but we live on. That's what we have to do, learn to live with this gaping hole in our hearts. This whole experience has shaped me into who I am, though. It's helped me to be a more empathetic and caring person. My siblings shaped me. I am proud to be their sister and wouldn't trade them for anything. I will always cherish the time I had with them and will continue to tell people about them because that's about all we can do to help them live on.

Marissa Williams

Me, and my sister, Kate.

My sister Kate,

$\mathcal{T}$he last time I talked to you, you said you were glad it was you and not me, as cancer took over your young body. Being 10 years old, I thought you were going to get better, and I often wonder if you thought the same.

The last time I saw you, you were gone. A part of me died with you that day.

I long for the days when we were kids, staying up late and laughing till it hurt. It's not fair I had to grow up without you, and to still, after all these years, watch mom suffer in silence...

I hate that my son will never know a second mother called aunt. He asks about you all the time, "Did Aunt Katie like ketchup? Or "Was Edward scissor hands her favorite movie?" So,

25

I tell him...all about you. Every single thing, every little memory. I cling to those, because it's the only way I know how to keep you with me. Because, honestly, it's the only thing I have left.

After all this time, I still feel you with me. Your light shines through in that little boy of mine—with his big blue eyes that are identical to yours. I know you sent him just for me.

It's been a long twenty years without you. I can't imagine twenty more. I have so much to tell you, but I have a feeling you already know.

I carry your smile and often speak your name, and I miss you with every breath I take.

Till we meet again, I'll be missing you.

Love

Carlie

My brother Justin and me.

The last time I saw you was one of the greatest days I ever spent with you. When I think of that day, all I remember is happy memories.

It was a day completely filled with your favorite things. We got Santiago's Mexican food and ate it in Washington Park. We drove around downtown Denver, which was your favorite place of all time. We went to the Denver Mint, and walked around the skyscraper district, where you felt the happiest. You showed me your apartment where you lived. I remember your abstract and modern style, with a real stop sign hanging in your entryway. I remember seeing happy pictures of you and your girlfriend, and amazing artwork that you created, and a life of yours that I never knew existed in that way but was too short-lived after the day I saw it. When you dropped me off, I was inclined to take a picture of you and your ever-so-loved car (as I was also eager to photograph almost everything in my life then). My aunt graciously wanted to take a picture of the both of us, and for that, I am forever grateful, because this was the last time I saw you.

Little did I know that you would be taken away from me nearly a month later.

At the young age of 16, I was starting to build my high school memories. I had my group of friends, my favorite styles, and plenty of classwork to keep me busy. It was my junior year, and I was ready to lead as an upperclassman, being 1st chair in the orchestra, spirit club president, and involved in too many other activities that kept grandpa busy taking me back and forth to school.

Labor Day weekend 2009 was planned with a pool party with all of my friends, until I received the call that forever changed my life.

I remember my grandma answering the phone call from my aunt. Once they handed the phone over to me, I knew something was not okay. All I remember hearing was "Justin was found dead in his apartment." I was so terrified, shocked, and devastated, I just screamed. I screamed at the top of my lungs for a long time, because I don't remember any more from that day.

In fact, I don't remember much from that point on. For more than a month in school, I was numb, going through the motions of student life. It's hard to remember how I was doing at the time, but I know it was the hardest thing I've ever experienced. I persevered with a difficult two years left of high school, and since then can reflect upon the stages of grief I have experienced in all of the changing times of my life. The pain that this caused has had the most significant impact on me. It's even very difficult to write this and relive the memories that make my heart hurt.

Though writing this is painful, I know that it will be cleansing and helpful to me. I'm so glad that I will be able to look back on this work and the works of others. Most of all, it will give a sense of mutual understanding between myself and other siblings that have lost their everything. It will bring me joy to read it over and over again, knowing that sharing my story for others to see was enlightening, or at the very least, made someone remember a memory of their sib and smile.

There isn't a day that goes by that I don't want to call you and tell you all about things in my life. There isn't a day that goes by that I don't miss you terribly. I've gotten your signs when you've visited me, and I'll keep you in my heart forever, JAF.

Chaeli Ferguson

The last time I saw you....

Dennis & Me (Jodee)
April 21st, 1996

$\mathcal{I}$t was a beautiful spring morning, sunny and cool. I had gotten up exceptionally early for a Sunday. Though I was sick with pleurisy, I had raised money and committed to walk for MS with my friend's mother who suffered with the disease. My younger sister, Danielle, and I were planning on meeting at the DiSario's home, so we could all ride into Boston together.

The morning started, as a typical Sunday did, with my father reading the paper, coffee in hand, and my mother at the sink doing dishes. As I sat down at the kitchen table, I noticed a duffel bag, belonging to my brother that had not been there the day before. A few months prior, Dennis had had a falling out with my parents, as many teenagers do, and temporarily moved in with a friend. It seemed he came home quietly during the night as we all slept. Happy and relieved that Dennis had finally returned, no one made a fuss when he stepped into the kitchen. It wasn't long before Dennis stepped outside with his dog.

Something made me look out the window.

I watched as he stood, almost eerily, staring out at the yard while petting Max. Moments later, I heard a car door. I walked outside and realized Dennis had left without a word. For reasons I did not understand at that moment, I was unusually upset that Dennis hadn't said goodbye.

It was as if he knew.

You could feel the excitement in the air as we lined up with hundreds, or perhaps thousands of others to march in the name of a cure for MS. Just as we got underway, we faintly heard someone yelling out in the crowd. We continued on, and the yelling became louder and clearer, "Is there a Jodee and Danielle McCarthy here?!" In a massive crowd of people in the middle of Boston, we never expected to hear our names, so without missing a beat, we continued. Again, we heard our names being called out, but this time we could see the officer shouting, there was no denying it. Confused, we all approached him. We were instructed to follow him. As we walked, he began to ask questions: did we have a sick or elderly relative? We kept walking until the officer lead us into a building. He approached a person standing in front of a podium. They quietly spoke a moment and then the officer handed me a phone and said, "Call this number or your brother in law, Jim." Still bewildered, I dialed the number. It was Milford Hospital.

My heart was suddenly racing. Unsure of what to say or who to ask to speak with, I immediately hung up. I began to think to myself, my brother-in-law is looking for us, we were given the number to our local hospital, dear God, something must have happened to my sister, my niece and nephew! Now I was panicked! I quickly dialed my sister's number.

Jim answered.

I could hear my voice quiver, "Jim, it's Jodee; what's wrong?" Silence...

"Dennis is dead."

I fell to my knees, dropping the phone, screaming, "NO! NO! NO!" Suddenly, I was sort of floating above, watching myself scream, cry, and sob uncontrollably. It was as if I was having an out-of-body-experience. People came running from all over to see what was happening. My poor sister, Danielle, immediately asked me, "What? What's wrong?" I couldn't even acknowledge her at that moment, I was not mentally present.

During the hour-long drive home, not a word was spoken by anyone. When we arrived, our front yard was filled with friends and relatives. It was true. DENNIS WAS DEAD. How could this be possible? He had finally come home. Dennis had just turned twenty. He had his whole life ahead of him, *his whole life.*

It's been twenty-two years since Dennis's death. As I write this, I relive it like it was just yesterday. No matter how many years go by, I will always miss and long for my brother. I imagine what life would be like if he had not died. I envision birthdays and holidays spent together. I can hear my children's laughter as their uncle Dennis does or says something funny. I see my sisters and me sitting with his wife, listening to her plan for his surprise 40th birthday party. I watch as all his friends' children grow into young adults, and I am curious what his kids would look like, how many he would have had. I wish my husband could have known Dennis. I know they would have laughed and joked together. I watch my parents, and it is physically painful to see how sad and lonely they have been without their baby boy. I pray to God there is an afterlife, if even only for a moment so we can tell Dennis how much we love him and how sorry we are that he had to die. For a very long time, as broken as we all were, I was more upset and worried that my brother was all alone, on the other side. At least we had each other here in the living world.

It haunted me.

To this day I cannot allow myself to TRULY think about how scared my brother must have been as he began to die. It's paralyzing to think he may have known his time was coming. I wonder if that's why he brought all his belongings home when he did; why he stood so long, staring into the yard, petting his dog one last time; why he snuck off that morning without saying goodbye. My heart aches for Dennis. As sad as I am for what all of us who knew Dennis missed out on, I am even more devastated at the thought of what he missed out on. It was HIS life that was cut short. I always feel guilty saying MY brother died, that's so selfish.

Dennis died.

Dennis died...

Jodee Maloney

Me (Joy) and my sister, Mary Ann Brookie.

*T*he last time I saw you, you were trying on your wedding dress. You had just stepped out of the dressing room, bashful but brimming with excitement. The entire area radiated with your happiness. It was a poignant moment full of unspoken word, filled with emotions only sisters could understand. We each were envisioning you on your wedding day, laughing, beautiful and surrounded by all our family. All the broken pieces would finally come together on that day to support you on your big day.

Our whole family.

We had been bonded our entire lives by the complexity of our parents' broken marriage. You lived with our mother, and I lived with our father. We grew up apart, but we were always connected. And on that day as you stood with the dappled sunlight casting sparkles over your dress, I was filled with love at the wonder of the woman you had become despite our embattled childhood. You had stepped out of the shadows of your very less than perfect youth and were poised on the brink of your own happily-ever-after.

But you never got the chance to step into that future.

After your death, I was left adrift. While you were alive, my place in both our families, although unhealthy, was set. I was your connector to our father's second family and you were my connector to our mother. We were these two individual intertwining pieces that held each other together in our separate and unequal families. We both knew what it felt like to feel unlovable because we had both been abandoned and unloved by a primary parent. We both knew what it felt like to have our other primary parent love, praise other children and partners above us. We knew how it felt to often be valued over those other children. We learned to take hits emotionally, monetarily and physically so that they wouldn't. We learned to love others and each other more than we loved ourselves. We knew what it felt like to get lost in our family and not really know whom we belonged to because we belonged to each other. So, it was okay, because we had each other to keep from drifting too far and getting too lost.

No matter how far I drifted or felt pulled under by life, you reminded me of how far I had swum and could go.

You believed in me like no other.

And I believed in you.

Together we were unsinkable. Now that you're gone, I often feel lost in the seas of my grief.

On the stormiest of these days, I think of you. I think of the last time I saw you, standing tall, dimples beaming, the sparkles of your wedding dress matching the sparkles in your eyes and I tearfully smile. Death can't steal that moment from us, because in that moment you always live for me, radiant, hopeful, filled with love and ready for the next step.

My beautiful Sister, Mary Ann Brookie, in her Wedding Dress

Loy Otto

Me, (Nicole) and my brother, Leon.

December 11, 2014 was the last time I heard my brother's laugh, encouraging words, and the extreme excitement in his voice as he was preparing for graduation.

It was one year ago today that he went home to be with the Lord.

The past year has been the hardest because when Leon died, my joy, hope, strength, dreams and visions died along with him. I was challenged in every area of my life spiritually, physically, and mentally but with much love, prayer, and support from others, I was able to overcome those challenges, and some I'm still overcoming.

If you have experienced the loss of a loved one or are grieving, here are some things that were learned/revealed/reconfirmed to me since my brother has passed:

-Although the hurt that I feel goes deep, God's love, grace, and mercy is much deeper!

-Grief is the celebration of the loss of a loved one through tears. It's the price you pay for loving others.

-There is no tragedy in being ushered from this life when the next life is spent in the presence of God. The only tragedy is a life that ends without that hope.

-When you love big, you lose big.

-In order to be strong, you have to be weak at times.

-God is real!

-I might not know all the answers to why Leon had to go, but I trust the one that does know...God...and I'm ok with that!

-*Despite the severity of our pain in any circumstance, God is still sovereign, and he knows what's best.* -Jeremiah 29:11

-*All our days are numbered, God knows our beginning and our end!* - Psalm 139:16

-One thing my brother always told me was to LIVE! We all must do that because each day is a gift, and *we are called to enjoy life and have it more abundantly.* John 10:10

-God has been able to use this situation to inspire me to do things I otherwise would have never done. Through that, God's been able to show me an even bigger purpose, bigger hope, and a greater joy that I never asked for, that I couldn't live without at this point in my life.

-This world is our temporary home, we are just passing through and we have an eternal home to prepare for, so we must be ready at ALL times! I'm not ready to die, but if I have to die, I *will* be ready.

I'm grateful that God has been restoring me, my faith, my visions and dreams, and for all the people, old and new he has placed in my family's life. As a doctor, I get the ability to help others heal and function better, and yet, God has been healing me in the process. I have gained *so many* sisters and brothers. Not only was I so proud of my brother graduating, but I loved his relationship with Christ. He always knew that God had him, he was a man of strong faith! So, some days when I'm crying, it's because I miss my brother's physical presence, his love, his support, his smile, his hugs, and him always being there for any big events that occurred, and the ones he will miss in the future. But I smile, because I know that I will see him again, that he's resting in the arms of Jesus, and I have so many memories to be thankful for. It's in those moments, I always remind myself of not only who Leon was, but WHOSE Leon was and that's as a child of the Most High! God made a deposit twenty-six years ago, a withdrawal three years ago, and now we are all are living on the interest :)

Love,

Nicole James Wilson

$\mathcal{T}$he last time I saw you was December 26, 2016.

I held your hand while your heart stopped beating. Now my precious and only baby brother, I hold you forever in my heart. Many siblings were not blessed the way we were. Born and raised in Des Plaines, IL, our childhood was filled with summer days at the park, pool, and pizza on speed dial. We rode our bikes, although you learned how to ride a two-wheeler before I did. We often played Hide and Seek throughout the neighborhood, hiding in the Sabarbaro's trees, down Marcel's basement window or in Jimmy's garage. My favorite time was on our playground swing set! I often wonder how many hours we clocked out there with Snoopy and Buddy. No wonder we were thin! At the end of the summer, we always took a family trip. I'll never forget you trying desperately to make the Queen of England's guards laugh. I truly believe they are the only ones that you didn't make laugh in this world. You certainly had that gift!

Once Ryan met someone, he took a genuine interest in their happiness immediately. Ry's smile lit up a room, however it was his caring heart that won anyone over. He's the guy who had his first girlfriend in kindergarten and remained friends with her throughout his life. His friendships lasted a lifetime as did the memories of him in costumes! It took a strong brave man to dress as a woman wearing pantyhose and heels or to wear a full-length, fuzzy, pink, bunny costume! He looked awesome!

Ryan Robert had more shoes than our mom and more watches than most millionaires. In fact, I remember each time we were at the mall, someone literally tried to buy Ry's purple shoes off his feet!

He cheered for all the Miami teams and was proud of his Irish/Polish heritage. Ryan was an innovative techie too.

I loved that Ryan and I attended so many sporting events together: The Super Bowl in Arizona, The Bulls Championship game in Chicago, and the first Brickyard 400 in Indy. My favorite event was watching Ryan and my dad drive race cars in Sebring!

Was there anything Ryan wouldn't do to make us smile? I don't think so. I remember one gloomy morning I just didn't want to go to work. I guess it was morning procrastination at its finest. Ryan saw a turtle moving faster than I was, and my typical smile was a dim frown. Ryan joined me in the kitchen. After locking eyes with me, he in what appeared like slow motion, poured his glass of ice water over his head with a straight face. I smiled and busted into laughter, asking what he was doing. He glared at me with a puzzled expression, as if standing in the middle of the kitchen in his boxers, drenched in freezing water with a puddle surrounding him was typical. That's my brother—he'd literally freeze to make me smile!

All I can say is, I don't know a man that had to endure as many medical challenges as he did. I certainly don't believe anyone could do so with the bravery and without complaints. You name it, sadly, Ryan had it. I would give my last breath at this very moment to save his life. I desperately miss sharing everything with him.

Ryan, please know, I will hold your hand in my heart forever and cherish our memories.

I love you!

Your Sister,

Lisa Rose
Flannery

(From left to right) are my sisters Adele and Emily, then me, Marie.

$\mathscr{T}$he last time I saw you was around your high school graduation. I was so incredibly proud of you, not for graduating high school, but for your decisions about attending college. You were so inspiring to me, to know what you wanted to do at such a young age and have the courage to do it. You were planning to move to San Francisco to pursue your dream of a career in fashion design. Although we have no family in California and you had only been there once, you seemed so certain and sure of what you were about to do. I love that you were following your passion so fearlessly.

We also met Austin at your graduation and got to know him a little. He was quiet during the ceremony but holding tight to the flowers he brought you. My impression was that he was a nice guy who really cared about you. At dinner a few days later, we got to spend more time with both of you, and I really liked him.

I had no idea that would be the last time I would see you, that in a couple of months you would both be gone. If I had known, I would have hugged you an extra time or maybe a little tighter. I remember being happy that night, but the details have faded. If I had known I would never see you again, I would have cemented every aspect of that night into my memory, everything you said, every time you laughed, every smile and expression.

Since you were 11 years younger than me, I don't remember fighting with you the way I did with Adele. When you were born, you were like a baby doll that could move, and we loved playing with you. It was such fun to watch you grow up, to see you learn to do things, and develop your own personality. You were only 6 when I went off to college, and you referred to the dorms as the dungeon because you wanted me to move back home. Some of my best memories with you were the times you came to stay with me in my apartment. We would eat ice cream and stay up late watching movies. One time when you were about 9 or 10, you told me that you thought you would be like me when you were older. I laughed because I was surprised that you would think of something like that as a child, but it was one of the best compliments I have ever received, and I will never forget it.

One of the last holidays we got to spend with you was Thanksgiving 2007. For some reason that year we decided to take a family picture to send out with Christmas cards, which I don't remember ever doing before that. We also wanted to take a picture of the three of us—you, me, and Adele. For some reason I also don't remember, we decided to take the picture laying on the bed instead of standing up. I think we were tired of standing and said if we all lay still, it would look the same as if we were standing, but of course it didn't. We got the giggles and that picture didn't turn out like we planned. It was so much better. We took some others standing up, but the picture on the bed is my favorite picture ever of all three of us. It was so typical of the way we could laugh hysterically about something no one else would understand.

Laughing with you is one of the things I miss the most.

Having you for a sister changed my life for the better. You continue to inspire me with your strong sense of self and confidence that I never had. You were so strong, whether you knew it or not. You were also so loving. It made my day when I would see you and your face would light up and you would run at me with a hug that only you could give. I know that when I get to Heaven, your face will light up and I'll get the best hug ever from you.

Love you all ways and always,

Your sister,

Marie

In my picture, I (Adele) am on the left and Emily (my sister) is on the right.

*T*he last time I saw you was at your graduation from high school. Or maybe it was a little while after that, but your graduation is the last time I remember seeing you now. If I had known it was going to be the last time I saw you, I would have made sure to remember everything about it. We thought you had your whole life ahead of you. No one expected you to leave us so soon.

I remember that you loved animals—especially horses. I remember that you used to hang out with your friends a lot, and you were also very connected with your family. I remember that you used to quote movies all the time, and you even said once that you saw a movie in the theater twice back-to-back and were quoting it the second time around.

I remember that you loved to travel, and you had plans to go to Paris with Marie, but that never happened, and now I don't think Marie wants to do it without you because I certainly wouldn't be able to fill your shoes on that trip.

I remember how, when you were little, and you got a new Disney movie, you used to watch the movie, rewind it, and watch it again, sometimes many times in a row. The Disney movies when you were little became part of the background of my life, and I think this may be a lot of the reason that I like Disney so much and want to work there.

I remember one time when Marie, you, and I were on a road trip that you waved at random people on the interstate and clapped and smiled and got so excited when they waved back.

I remember when you were little, and you liked to play the guessing game at dinner where everyone had to guess how many beans would be in your green bean before you opened it and then ate it. Marie and I would often guess completely unrealistic numbers like in the hundreds, and we even also liked to guess the numbers PI and infinity. You weren't phased by it and would excitedly announce, "No! It's THREE!" I also remember you saying later that you were confused at the time, but when you learned about PI in math at school, you were like "Ooooh! Now I get it."

I remember so many things about your life. There are so many happy memories. The thing that sucks the most is that we don't get any more memories of or with you. That is the worst part of losing someone you love...you lose all the future moments that you should have had.

Love always and all ways,

54

Sylvia & her brother, John Paul German (Johnny)

*T*he last time I saw you was May 17, 2016, the worst day of our lives. You were dying. I don't know if you knew I was there, but I held you and played you one of our favorite songs.

When I was first given the opportunity to write something about you that would be shared with others, I knew there was no way I could pass up such a blessing. I think about you all the time. I love to talk about you.

The thing is, I don't have one favorite memory of you. I cherish each and every one. Remember that time Aunt Jennie took us to Magic Mountain and we got lost? We tried to cross that rope bridge, but it seemed so high and scary. I'll bet it was tiny, but so were we.

That's the thing about losing a sibling, losing you. We were only one year apart and always together. I never realized before you died how much of my identity and life story was inextricably wound with you. You are my past and were supposed to be my future. Now, so many of my memories cannot be reminisced on with the other key player. Only I can tell the story, you aren't here to back me up and add your own nuance.

Sylvia and her brothers, Johnny and Jimmy.

Maybe you'd remember how we found Aunt Jennie that day. I can't remember how the story ends. I just remember not being very scared because I was with you, my best friend. It felt like an adventure. I love remembering being with you.

I can tell people about you all day. That you were smart, and funny and loving. That you could beat any video game and fix any electronic thing you encountered. That you couldn't sing but did it anyway, loud and happy. You made fun of my name and were better at picking on me than I was at picking on you. I'd give up a lot, to have you right here, calling me Saliva, as much as I hated it when you were alive.

You loved your family and would have done anything for us. I think you'd give up heaven to come back to us and ease our pain. I can say all these things, but they are a poor substitute for you. If people could meet you, they'd know it's all true. You weren't a saint, of course.

You had your issues and they drove me insane when you were here. We let our problems get in the way and I'll always regret that we didn't spend more time together in the last couple of years before you died.

Since the day you died, I have wished I could be with you. Somewhere. Anywhere.

Candid photos where you were just there, a casual part of my life, make me so sad. As my big brother you were always there, a given.

Part of my life.

Now you're gone.

Everything reminds me of you. Music, movies, food, streets, lakes, hiking. Everything. I can't help but look for you in everything I do and everywhere I go. And I find you. You are everywhere. I take you with me always. I love you.

And I'll miss you until the day I die.

Love always,

Sylvia

Johnny, Stephanie, Sylvia and Jimmy

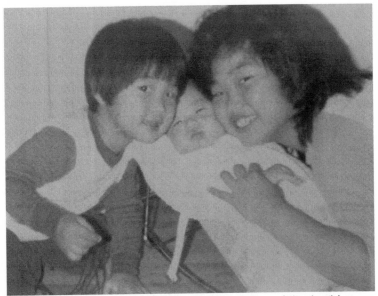

My brothers, Tommy, Jimmy Kim, and me (Elizabeth)

Introduction

For those of you reading this excerpt, we most likely share a common bond. We have lost someone we love and the ache we feel is heartbreaking. My brother's name was Jimmy Kim, and he was only 32 years old.

On May 10, 2016, he passed away from a massive brain hemorrhage and left a huge hole in my heart and my life. In true fashion of his generosity, his heart, liver and kidneys were donated. Because of his thoughtfulness, 3 people were able to have a second chance at life.

When we were younger, times tough and me being 7 years older I raised him and took care of him as both our parents worked long and hard to provide a home and food to eat. Jimmy was a big man at six-foot-tall and 300 pounds, but he was still my baby brother and my world. He was a pastry chef by trade, and suffered from Quadequina Syndrome, a severe neurological condition which left him in great pain in the latter part of his life. He was a sassy giant, quick witted and full of humor. Initially, I asked myself how I was going to continue with a normal life. How could I make things go back to the way it used to be? Now I realize that it will never be the way it was. I am learning that I must make and accept a new normal without my brother. The following is like a letter to my late brother, Jimmy Kim.

The first and the last

"I'm telling!"

"Don't touch me!"

"But I'm not touching you!"

"Why are you bothering me?"

If I had known then what I know now, I would have told you and Tommy that all that sibling banter was just a term of endearment. *What I would give to go back to that time…*

I don't remember the first time I met you, but I do remember the first tears I had for you. I recall seeing your little body in an incubator because you were severely jaundiced. They had to perform a complete blood transfusion and you looked so sickly to me, but the love I had for you was so overwhelming and at age seven I felt what true love really was. I recall telling mom you weren't sleeping well, and she didn't believe me, until we took you to the ENT. They did a sleep study on you and you were not breathing for as long as 60 seconds at a time because you had obstructive sleep apnea. I was there, again to hold your hand through your first surgery when they had to remove your tonsils and adenoids. Remember the first time I had to fight my battle with cancer? You assured me that everything would be okay and that I needed to concentrate on looking towards the future because people relied on me. I drew strength from you.

You had all my firsts throughout my childhood and my adulthood. I had many highs and lows, and, at every step, the constant was you. When I thought I had my first love, you were right there to tell me to wake up and smell the coffee. When I had my first job, you were there to congratulate me with a really nice dinner. When I had my first child, you were there supporting me with everything a pregnant sister would ever need. After the birth of your nephew, you stepped in as the best uncle a child could ever have.

Since you passed, I often wondered what you would say to me as I traveled through life. I wondered what you would say as I try to find a new norm without you. I think that's what I miss the most about you in that whatever I did or decided to do, you listened, gave me your opinion and just supported me through and through with no hesitation and no judgment.

The last time I physically saw you was to confirm your body at the funeral home. I have tried to recall the last time I heard your voice, but all I can do now is replay a video of your laughter from our last vacation together at Universal Studios. Through it all, there are so many lessons that I am still learning. Be kind to one another. Show the ones you care about just how much you really care, not just with words but with actions. Remember that you can't take the physical world with you when you depart from this Earth, but you can leave a lifetime of memories to those you leave behind.

Elizabeth

Sam Shelton (3/11/97 – 1/26/16)

The last time I saw you was a week or so before Halloween 2015. I came to visit you at your college, and we got lunch, then walked Pearl Street looking for Halloween costume materials at thrift shops. I was 23, you 18, but you joked with the waitress that my ID was fake when I ordered a beer. I don't remember what clothes you tried on in the thrift shops, but I remember the laughter, the sun, the easy happiness.

I dropped you off at your dorm, we hugged goodbye, and then I drove 40 minutes back to my place. There was no way to know that was going to be the last time.

But, then again, we all know that wasn't really the last time. To say that was the last time is to omit the 10 weeks in the hospital when I saw you every day. I spent more cumulative time with you during the hospital weeks than the last 5 years combined. And I value that time, because it was so focused on you. Talking about you, talking to you, meeting your friends who visited, reading the dozens of pieces of mail you received weekly, explaining you to the doctors, discovering your secret tattoos— it was the most meaningful time in my life. But I don't count it as the last time I saw you, because I refuse to let the comatose version of you serve as my final memory.

Instead, I hold on to other "lasts." The last time at college, of course, is huge, but there's another major last: the last family vacation. Memories of that vacation pop into my mind every day. I think of the four of us at dinner in Portugal laughing. I see you, moments after arriving, running through the park in Vigo, jumping off stone walls and scampering around the ruins of the fort. I recall climbing to the top of the tower in Lisbon while our parents went to the art museum, and then wandering around trying to figure out how to find them without working cellphones. I smile, remembering when Mom realized we'd left our passports behind, 30 minutes after driving out of Lisbon, and she turned the car around, while you and I attempted to whistle songs in harmony in the backseat. We'd whistle three or four notes and then collapse into giggles. Everything about that last trip felt, ironically, like a beginning. It was the first time our family traveled like that together—as adults who enjoyed just sitting and eating and drinking and talking together, no need for kid activities. There was the promise of more trips like that. I was so sure they would happen.

Hanging onto these last memories preserves you as the lively, genuine, gregarious person you were before the crash. I feel lucky that your final months of true life, before the hospital, were so positive and conflict-free.

Halloween is a few weeks away as I write this, which must mean we're close to the second anniversary of the last time I saw you. It might even be today. I could go back in our text message history and figure out exactly when it was, but I don't want to. The date of the crash is hard, the date of your death is hard, your birthday is hard, Christmas is hard—I'm not going to add to all of that.

The last time I saw you truly alive was in October, and the last time I saw your body was the following January. Still, there's one more way you remain constantly, vividly present and changing: in dreams. In dreams, I get to see you as a baby sitting on my lap or a teenager running through a field. Sometimes you're not yourself—you can't speak, or your head is wrapped in bandages—but even *those* dreams are welcomed. They're new and they're you, and they always make me wake up with a smile on my face.

You didn't have to die. You didn't want to die. You could have never seen this coming. But I'm thankful that you lived the way you did, because it left a mark. Everyone who knew you remembers their last time with you, and I'm willing to bet that 99% of those memories were positive. Our time with you was a gift. Thank you.

Clara Shelton

My Brother, Scott

My daughter, Madi, me, (Pam) and my brother, Scott

I don't know many families that were as close as my family. In fact, I don't know any! I'm not insinuating that we were perfect or that there weren't any problems. But the close relationships we had between each other grew over the years, unlike some who lose contact as they go on with their lives. I was blessed with a mom and dad that raised my brother and me with good morals, and manners, and taught us what unconditional love was.

My brother, Brian Scott, Walker, had always been my protector. Even when we were little kids I felt a sense of security, knowing my brother was by my side. (The truth is we were only 3 years apart)

He was patient and wonderful at playing with me. As we grew a little bit older, there was that awkward phase of me embarrassing him in front of his friends. He was a skater and would often come home to find my BFF and me in the loft of his

67

room playing Barbie's, my *New Kids on the Block* posters everywhere.

Despite it all, he still loved me.

I'm sure I got on his nerves. In fact, I know I did. I admit that I used to sneak into his room when he wasn't home and look through the bottom drawer of his dresser to see what I could find. I never intended to get him in trouble. I was just curious. (Okay, more like nosy) he eventually started locking his door and would use a toothpick to open it.

But he never stopped loving me, and within minutes after being irritated, he was his loving, protective self again.

Every summer we took a family car trip to my mom's hometown of Smithville, Texas, to visit our Grandparents and Uncle Jerry. I have so many wonderful memories from those trips. Playing games in the car with Scott, building houses with Lincoln Logs, swimming in the little inflatable pool, and going fishing. The best was laughing our heads off at my dad, and the silly things he would say and do.

Then there were the bad memories—when our first dog, Benji, died. I remember Scott hugging me and us crying uncontrollably. There were many times when my dad was in the hospital and, although he was scared too, Scott would put his arm around me and reassure me that everything was going to be okay.

As we grew up a little bit more, I began to envy him. I don't think he had any clue (I wish I could go back in time and tell him).

I thought the way he dressed, the way he talked, the music he listened to, everything he did was "cool". I remember this one time that I wore his black jacket with the zippers all over and the converse high-tops. Then there was the time I wore the green plaid shorts just like his (come to think of it, I think they *were* his!)

When he started driving, I loved for him to take me with him. Not so I could go where I wanted, but so people could see me in his rad car. He had built a wall with huge loud speakers that blew out your ear drums. It was all about the bass back in the day.

He tried to teach me how to drive stick. I still remember sitting in his white, *Suzuki Swift,* trying to get the hang of the clutch, him laughing hysterically.

As young adults, my brother was still my protector, and he loved to do things for me. He would take my car up to the gate store to put gas in it. He would surprise me with a Monster *Energy Drink*. He was always looking at my car and saying things like, we need to get air in your tires or I need to change your oil. Then there was the time he found my future husband's wet swimming shorts in the trunk of my red *Hyundai.* He gave me a look like he did not approve and said I needed to be careful! *That was my brother.*

Once I got married, moved to Tampa and had a daughter, we remained close but didn't get to see each other as often. He worked so many hours and had a hard time getting time off to come to Tampa. My daughter, Madison, and I took trips to Jacksonville as often as we could. My dad's health had begun to decline, and my mom didn't have a choice but to put him in a nursing home. Scott remained loyal to his dad. He drove to Green Cove Springs every night after he got off work and spent hours sitting by my dad's side. He cleaned his mouth out. He suctioned him. He played his favorite songs. My dad's face lit up every time he saw my brother. You can imagine the pain and suffering us all experienced when my dad passed away on January 12, 2016.

My brother lost his hero. But he continued to help others and love his mom and sis.

He and my daughter, Madison, became closer than anything. He loved her like his own child. He loved to play with her, spoil her and simply spend time with her. I can picture him flying her through the air like superman, watching fireworks from his apartment, the excitement on his face when she opened his presents at Christmas.

The last time I saw my brother was the week of Thanksgiving. He and my mom had come to Tampa to spend the week/weekend with us. Thanksgiving was good, and every moment we had together was special.

Then my world came crashing down.

On December 6, 2016 I got a phone call from my mom that Orange Park Hospital had called and said that her son was in the ER! I never imagined losing my brother.

At that moment, I just thought he had been in an accident, perhaps was really injured. I sat and rocked back and forth and prayed "Dear God, please take care of my brother." After about 45 minutes, my mom called back and in a very soft voice said "Pam, he's gone". That is the day my brother and best friend left this Earth. And my heart will never be the same.

I miss you, and will always love you, Scott!

I look forward to the day when we will see each other again.

Love,

Your little sis,

Pam

Scott & Madi

Me (Lynelle) & My Brother, Kevin

$\mathscr{T}$he last time I saw you was the day before you were cremated.

That was the day I completely lost it, and realized you were truly gone. I walked into the room and saw you lying there so peacefully. How can that be when my life was crumbling right in front of me? This must be a nightmare.

My brother, my friend was gone.

You weren't supposed to be gone. You had just proposed to your girlfriend the night before you died. You see, for the people reading this, my brother had autism and suffered from mental illness. By looking at him, you would have never known he was autistic. Autism is not what haunted him, but his mental illness did, and it started when he was in high school. Despite this, he succeeded in inspiring and encouraging those around him, even during his darkest moments.

71

He was quick to offer a helping hand to those in need, he would talk to the homeless because he understood their struggles, he would give anyone a big teddy bear hug when they were having a bad day or try to get them to smile with a corny joke. However, on December 31, 2008 he died tragically. The group home he lived in had given him medication that was not prescribed to him, and he had a lethal reaction. *How could my twenty-five-year-old brother be gone? Who was going to listen to my crazy stories? Who was going to make me laugh when I was having a bad day? Who was going to call me every day to check on me?*

My brother and I were very close. My brother was very quiet, and did not trust people very easily, so therefore felt he did not have many friends, but merely acquaintances. The day of his memorial service over two-hundred people showed up to pay their respects, some of them standing in the parking lot because the funeral home was full. Not only did he leave an impact on me forever, but he also left an impact on the people whose lives he touched.

Although he was taken from us tragically, I know he is always with me. My brother, my friend, not only showed me what love truly is, but taught me how not judge a book by its cover. He made me realize that even though someone is homeless, or having a hard time in life, they are still a human being with feelings and worth something. He taught me that there are many ways to roll a cigarette, and all the ways you can cuss. He taught me about music that I would never, in a million years, listen to. But most importantly what he taught me was to be secure in who I am, and not let what other people think interfere with that. Although I am still working on that, it is something I continue to strive for. I know he is not coming back and that's what hurts the most. I can still hear his laugh, see his smile, and remember his hugs. So, I will end with this:

Kevin, the hardest part of losing you is trying to figure out how to live without you. I want you to know that there is never a day that goes by that I don't think of you. I know I will see you again, but until then, just keep watching over us, sending feathers, and know that I love you.

Lynelle Sturgeon

Dearest Sully,

I am not even sure where to begin as I have so many things on my mind, but "I miss you terribly" seems like an appropriate start...

If anyone had told me that this would be life right now, I would have laughed in their face. When mum called and said "you need to come to the hospital, they don't think he will make it through the night" ... I remember thinking it was a bad dream. Upon seeing you, lifeless in the trauma room, with tubes and blood, your clothes cut on the floor, I knew then it was real. Listening to the doctor tell us how sorry he was, that there wasn't anything else they could do as he had "never in all his years seen a brain MRI so terrible on the initial scan" were simply words I couldn't comprehend. *How could this be happening? Why?* You finally seemed happy, your life was coming together and then you were dying right before my eyes.

The next thirty or so hours you remained on life support was horrific. I didn't know whether to tell you to fight to live or that it was okay to go. I wanted to tell you how much I needed you, how much I loved you and even though you had been a huge pain in my ass that I couldn't do this life without you. I wanted to tell you that you were a wonderful brother, a great son and a terrific father... We know it wasn't always "you" doing hurtful things. I should have told you that I was so sorry for not doing more, for eventually having to let you face struggles on your own because I had my two babies, and I mentally couldn't do it anymore.

You had been my inspiration for recovery and getting mental health treatment and I couldn't save you.

I wanted to tell you all of this and more, but the words wouldn't come and all I could say was "I love you, Sully."

Watching you take your last breath was something I will never forget. My heart broke that day and pieces of it went to

Heaven with you. All the amazing memories we shared, the rough times, laughs, cries and every single thing that use to annoy me about you became something I longed for. I knew OUR birthday would never be the same, holidays would never be the same and our mother would never be the same. I had to look your daughter in the face and tell her that her daddy was gone. It makes me physically ill thinking about it. It wasn't fair that my kids wouldn't know you, that your daughter would walk through life without you, that Mark and I were burying our brother and that your parents had lost their first-born son. We got through it, together, as a family.

Life was so hard after that; I felt broken and empty. Mum and I would go to the cemetery every single day. To see the pain she carried killed me, but she pushed on for her grand babies. When mum was diagnosed with cancer, I knew she wouldn't survive because she wanted to be with you, in Heaven. The evening of your second anniversary, as I sat with our dying mother I assured her how much I loved her, and that Mark and I would be okay. Just like that, she was gone. Cancer had taken her in eight short months, the day after your anniversary. Never did I think I would be without both of you, but what a beautiful reunion that must have been, mother and son together once again. Thirty days later, Auntie came to join you both... on OUR birthday. I had no clue that, in the two years since you passed, I would bury five of my closest family members.

To say I am a different person would be an understatement.

I believe, with everything in me, that things happen for a reason. I know you're at peace, you're where you need to be, but I'm still not happy about it. My heart seems empty, my soul hollow and I seldom "feel" anything. I have learned to accept that this is in fact "life" now, but some days are just so hard. I sometimes forget what your voice sounded like, but I remember other things. Your obsessive fingernail cutting, singing, bear hugs and the way you smelled. I sometimes still smell your cologne randomly and it brings me great comfort. I remember your kindness and even when there were times you didn't have much of anything, you would give someone the shirt off your back! I remember how much we were alike, emotionally, and everyone said we were "too sentimental." I remember the love you had for your daughter, for my kids, for everyone really but you never felt "good enough" even though you were MORE than enough. I remember how broken you were, and you use to hide it well and then you just gave up on hiding it.

I hope you remember how much you were truly and sincerely loved and adored, and I hope you know how much you are missed each and every day.

Paul Joseph, simply thinking about you breaks my heart all over again. When I dreamt of you one night and we were in the car and I looked at you and said, "I can't believe you're gonna be gone soon," and you replied "I know, but it will all be okay." I don't know when and I don't know how, but I know it will be okay. Please continue watching over your baby girl and my kids. They talk about you all the time, it's incredible. Tell Mum, Bev and everyone else I say hello. I know it was hard for Mum to leave but let her know it's okay, we are okay because I know she is where she needs to be. We will have one hell of a party when I come home to Heaven.

Thank you, Sully, for teaching me how to live through your death, for holding me up in the times I was sure I would crumble, for loving me when I was unlovable and for being the best brother and friend I could ask for. I hope I make you proud. Until we meet again, remember how much I love and miss you.

Love forever,

Ling Ling

(Lisa Corvi Suarez)

In loving memory of
Paul Joseph Sullivan
1.28.71 - 12.28.14

The Last Time I saw You

*T*he last time I saw you

you were a shadow of your former self, an empty shell

The last time I saw you

you were taking your final breaths

The last time I saw you

they took you away from me in a body bag

I thought I would never ever

get those images out of my head

So, I would rather not like to think about

the last time I saw you.

I would rather like to think about

our growing up together

you were the middle child

you were the first to take liberties and push boundaries

I just loved your free and adventurous spirit so much!

I would rather like to think about

Your incredible charisma

Three sisters, from left to right

(Youngest to oldest): Sabine, Petra, Ellen

so much charisma that it would just ooze out of you

You had the ability to go into a noisy crowded room

and have everyone go quiet when you entered

with every man looking at you

It was remarkable.

I would rather like to think about

your kindness

your giving and generous nature

always giving to others

rescuing others, human and animal.

So, giving that you would give anyone

your last dollar or the shirt on your back.

I would rather like to think about

so many special times we shared

The Christmases we spent together

Unfortunately, there were only few in adulthood

I would rather like to think about

all our lovely visits back & forth

and our time together in fun places like

San Francisco, Vancouver, Seattle, and Orcas Island.

I am so grateful for all the time we got to spend together

I wish it could have been more.

The last time I saw you

you saved my life

when I was in a 190 miles per hour head on car crash

It is the only explanation that makes sense

as to why I am still here.

The last time I saw you

you visited me in my dreams

and we were able to spend time together

I cannot tell you how much I appreciate your visits.

I hope you come again soon.

The last time I saw you

you came to me as a beautiful animal

lingering much too close and for far too long

because you know how much I love animals

and would take notice.

The last time I saw you

you were everywhere

inside and outside of me

and all around me

of that I am certain.

We may be separated by a veil

But you are always here with me

Now and Forever.

By *Sabine Jordan* 2017

For Petra Steinbrück/Dickinson/Melton/Jurries (1962-1999)

Petra with her two children Jack and Brian, and third husband on a visit at my coastal enclave near San Francisco

The Last Time I Saw You

My brother, Chris

*T*he last time I saw you was in a dream. We were in the living room of our Mother's childhood home. The large mountain oil painting and plush mauve reclining La-Z-Boy chairs were just the same in my dream as they were when we visited growing up.

I was sitting in one of the recliners, and you were in the other. In my mind, I knew it wasn't your birthday, but I wished you Happy Birthday and said, "I want you to be happy," with all the sincerity I had.

We got up, and you gave me the best hug. It was a long hug. I could feel your strong muscles in your back from doing carpentry. I pressed my head into your chest as we embraced. I felt the love we shared for each other.

Then I awoke.

The last time I saw my brother, Chris, *alive* was during the weekend of a family wedding in the month of June. I lived out of state in North Dakota, worked for my alma mater, Colorado State University. I was part of a team doing field research with wild horses in Theodore Roosevelt National Park.

I came home to my parents' place and we drove down to Iowa together. Chris and a St. Paul cousin drove down together on a whim, in a rented compact, luxury sports car. I recall him saying how much he enjoyed the drive.

Chris and I hadn't seen each other in months, maybe even since Christmas. The day of the wedding, Chris wanted to get his hair cut. I went with him. We talked about tattoos, music, and the relationships we were in. While Chris was in the barber chair, some disturbing news coverage came on the TV. Our eyes locked. Chris had fallen victim to a similar situation. I should have asked the barber to change the channel. I didn't. I wish I had said some supportive words to him as we left the barber shop, but I didn't.

Back at the hotel, I couldn't decide what dress to wear, due to sunburn and ugly tan lines. *Nope, the yellow one won't work, but the blue one will*. I had music playing on my Ipod. "Shout" by *The Temptations*. We were both in playful moods. He started dancing to the song, and I joined in. Several feet apart, we were facing each other, doing a combination of the twist with jazz hands raised in the air. Each time we heard the word SHOUT he'd do a 180 degree jump in the air. I couldn't resist and joined in as well!

At the wedding reception, I saw my brother do something he rarely did...he worked the crowd. He was going around talking to all our cousins. He looked handsome and comfortable in his own skin. He handed out hugs, there were big smiles and laughter all around. He carpooled back with my parents and me after the wedding. He was silly, joking nearly the whole four hours home. Every few miles, he would talk in a new accent and bust out a one-liner. It was one of those times my belly hurt from laughing so much and my cheeks were sore from smiling.

I would like to say the drive home from the wedding was the last time I saw my brother Chris alive, but it wasn't.

At the end of that weekend he was rushing off to see his girlfriend. He hopped in his big, red Chevy truck, had it in drive, foot on the break, and I walked out to meet him. "Bye, Mag – Bye, Bubbie." No hug. No love ya.

I never thought I'd never see him alive again.

That was the last time I saw my beloved big brother, mentor, confidant, and only sibling alive.

Maggie Bauer

Michael Steven Duncan

1963-2005

Lori Ann Duncan and her brother, Michael Steven Duncan.

(This picture was taken on my birthday when I was 24 and Michael was 21. It isn't recent of course but it is my favorite picture of us.)

*M*ichael was my little brother, my best friend, my hero, and my confidante for forty-two years. He was my only sibling.

When my brother was diagnosed with Stage 4 Multiple Myeloma on August 20, 2005, I had no idea he only had four more months to live. I had no idea that the last day I spent with him would be his last on this earth.

The morning of December 20, 2005 started out with my daily visit to my brother who had been hospitalized for the past few weeks. The doctors met with my family around noon and told us he wouldn't last through the day. I immediately went home and got his Christmas present—a 49ers blanket, because my brother was a die-hard 49ers fan since he was old enough to know what football was. He opened my present and told his wife to take it home and he would enjoy it once he got better. (My brother was buried with this blanket).

Michael never gave up hope and wanted to make sure we didn't either. I spent the entire day with him until around 9 pm when the doctors told us it looked like he would make it through the night. I kissed him, told him I loved him, and I would see him tomorrow. At 10:30 that night I got call from my sister-in-law saying to get to the hospital.

I got there in time to hold his hand, tell him I loved him, and that everything would be okay. I told him not to worry, that I would make sure Mom and Dad and his kids would be okay.

Michael took his last breath five minutes after I got there.

I know he was waiting for me. I sat with my only sibling, my beloved brother for about thirty minutes after he died.

Just me and Michael.

So many precious memories ran through my mind: our childhood, our teen-age years, our adult years as parents and aunt and uncle to each other's children. Those memories are the most painful yet the most beloved memories of my life. My brother has been gone almost 12 years and there is not a day that goes by that I do not think of him and miss him with every ounce of my being.

I know I will see you again someday, Michael. I love you and miss you forever.

Lori Ann Duncan

My sister, Jillian, and Me (Marissa)

$\mathcal{M}$y name is Marissa Casey, and I was fourteen when I lost my sister.

My sister was named Jillian Lee Baker. She was eleven years older than me, and she was my biggest role model. Jill died by suicide on May 8th, 2013.

I remember the last time I talked to Jill as if it happened yesterday. It was just two days before she took her own life. She died on a Wednesday; why I can still remember that, who knows. I called her as I came home the Monday before, wanting to vent about something. She informed me that I had just missed her as she just left my house. I remember fourteen-year- old me feeling so angry that I didn't get to see her. I begged for her to her turn around, but promised she'd see me on Friday.

A promise she failed to deliver by twos days, but I never held that against her.

However, to this day, I have never spoken about our last phone conversation to another. It hurts too much to know that if I had left my friend's house a little earlier, I could have seen her face one last time before seeing her in a box.

Jill and I used to have movie night every Friday when she still lived at home. We would eat and put in a movie. Jill loved Twilight, so she and I watched it religiously. Jill died before I saw the last one, and to this day, I can't watch it. It's almost as if I finish it without her, the last thing connecting her to me will disappear. I own the DVD and I stare at it sometimes, but I have never gotten myself to put it in and press play.

It's almost as if right before I push that button, she wipers in my ear "Really, you asshole, you're gonna watch our movie without me?"

It's hard for me to remember her completely; whether it's because it hurts too much or maybe I was too young to appreciate our time enough to remember things. I don't know.

I do remember, though, Jill being my favorite person. The only person in the world that I wanted to talk to when I was sad and the only person I felt I could truly open up to.

Jill always got me out of trouble. I remember one time I didn't do a school project, and I forced her to do it with me. It was the best day of my fifth-grade life. We baked a cake for the project and made the biggest mess in the kitchen. It was covered in frosting but filled with love. I also remember we tried to catch a bat with a sock and an apple and, instead of tossing the apple in the air like she was supposed to, she accidentally knocked it into woods and I owed laughed so hard.

To this day, I've never met anyone whose friendship even compared to Jill's. She is my best friend and always will be. I was the first person in my grade to experience a "tragic loss". There were a few kids who lost a grandparent, but nothing quite like what I went through. I grew up in a small town, so word got around quick. I would walk down the hallway, and kids would either stare at me or try their hardest not to look at me, and I didn't blame them. Had it been the other way around, I would

94

have stared too. I was the girl *"Whose sister killed herself"*. No one in my grade had really dealt with a classmate losing someone, let alone a suicide.

I thought Jill dying made me feel alone, but then going back to school and realizing how "fucked up" I was to everyone else made it even worse. No one would really talk to me. I remember my sophomore year of high school. There was a girl in my school who lost her sister in a car accident and, as if people forgot about what happened, to which the probably did, whispered things about her to me like "How is she laughing with friends if her sister died? Don't you think she should be crying?" Little do they know, she was upset—just not to the uneducated eyes. I wanted so desperately to go up to her and tell her that I feel her pain and give my number, so she had someone to talk to, and for whatever reason, I never did and that's still my biggest regret to this day.

Jill will always be my biggest smile, but my worst pain. She made my small, preteen world go round, and losing her nearly killed me too, but I forced myself to go on. The whole saying "It gets easier" is bull shit. You just learn how to live with it better. Sometimes you're alright, but other times your world comes crashing down around you, and that's ok because it's part or grieving.

My world will never be the same without Jill.

Marissa Casey

Barry,

$\mathcal{I}$t's been one month since you left.

My heart aches most of the time. There are too many things I have to do each day that we would do together. Every day, there seems to be a new "first" for me. I know you wouldn't want me dwelling on the fact that you're gone, so I'll try to do better.

I wish I wouldn't have missed the phone call from NMC telling me that something had happened. I feel so guilty about that. I hate that no one was at the hospital for you. I should have been there. I hate that you were alone, and I'm sorry. I do know that it was God who made me miss the call. Mom said it was so nice to have their pastor there when they got the news. That wouldn't have happened if I had taken that call. So, in that respect, I'm glad how things worked out.

I wanted to say goodbye and tell you how GREAT it was having you around. I was trying to prepare myself for when you moved out, but this just threw me for a loop! It's not fair. I now have to adjust to my "new" normal.

Saturdays are so hard. We had so much fun when you were here. I'm sitting on the patio on a perfect spring night. I know we would have a fire going and just talking...about EVERYTHING.

I miss you, and I always will.

I love you, and I always will.

When my time comes, YOU better be the first to greet me in Heaven! I'm looking forward to that.

Miss you, my brother,

Jerolyn

PS...Sas misses you, too

Barry A. Stutzman 12/2/1972-3/20/2017

Dave and me (Ales)

$\mathscr{T}$he last time I saw you was the weekend before you died.

You sent me a message asking if I was watching the fight. I answered, "What fight?" My brother's reply was, "It's only the biggest fight of the century. Floyd Mayweather Vs Manny

99

Pacquiao". He had been working all week and had lots of money, so he booked a return four-hour bus journey and arrived in the afternoon. He was his usually cheery self. He was a big lad and towered over me. I asked him what he'd been up to, but he seemed quite vague. We drank some beers and watched boxing; we cheered we laughed, and it was a fun night.

As kids, my brother Dave and I had fought like typical brothers and sisters did. We argued, we got each other into trouble, but as we grew older our relationship changed. We grew closer and closer. We enjoyed each other's company. We talked about music.

Dave was three years younger than me, and he was thirty-six years old when he passed.

We had a mostly-happy childhood until our parents divorced. There were some things I wish I had done differently; maybe if I hadn't moved to a different city, he would still be here.

My brother had a relationship and became a father to two beautiful children. The year he died he had just become a dad again with another gorgeous son. It makes me sad that he won't know what a great dad he would've been.

My teenage son adored his Uncle Dave. They arm-wrestled one night which I recorded on my phone, and I'm so happy I did. My son knew he couldn't win, so he cheated and used his body weight. In the video, Dave and Max are laughing hysterically. It's a memory that I'll cherish forever as I can at least listen to his voice.

The things I miss the most about my brother are his amazing sense of humor, his smile and his laugh. He always made me laugh, and he knew me better than anyone in my family. We shared secrets, we went out to gigs, we went on holiday together and we enjoyed each other's company. It was comforting when he was around me. I felt loved, needed. I had a purpose.

I'll never forget the phone call that changed my life forever. It was the most devastating news. My dad told me. It took my breath away—always does when I think about it.

I miss you, Dave, and I love you and I wish I could've done more to help you. I did try; it just wasn't enough. See you over the rainbow.

Love always,

Your big sis, *Ales*

Xxx

My son, Max, and my brother Dave.

Below, Dave and I as young kids

Megan and Me (Michele)

April 14th, 2015 around 5pm, I got the phone call that forever changed my life.

I will never forget the phone call or my mom's tone as she said, "Megan is dead".

All I could say was, "What do you mean?" I had just Face-Timed with her the night before. It's weird how life works and the signs you receive without even thinking about it. I was having the worst day that day, too. Nothing was going right. Looking back, they were signs from Megan that something was wrong. It tears me up inside, because what if she just would've called me instead of her friend.

Maybe she'd still be here.

*M*egan was a wonderful person. She was funny, and always took care of everyone she loved. Her laugh was contagious, and she always had a smile on her face.

And I know she adored me.

She was my baby sister, and I wasn't always the best sister, but to her I was the one she looked up to. I can't tell you how much I miss her or her smile, or all the memories we've shared, or how she was the only one I want to call when something happens because she was and is the only one that will understand.

I was thirty weeks pregnant with my twins when she died, and I know she would've loved them to death. Now, I know they have a guardian angel watching over them.

As the time goes, it's easier to deal with, but the pain is always there. If I know I'm going to be talking about Megan I can hold back my tears, but if someone catches me off guard I know I won't be able to hold back. If people don't know Megan, I feel like I have to explain that Megan was a great person before they know she died from a heroin overdose. She wasn't her addiction, she was a great person who got caught up in some bad decisions.

The Last Time I Saw Megan was on March 28th, 2015. I came back to my hometown for my baby shower that was held the next day. My sister wouldn't be able to come because she was on the bracelet and couldn't get permission to go, but I still wanted to see her. Our mom and I went to her work, *Applebees*. I just got my haircut, so she came over with a big smile on her face and touched my hair and said she liked it. I remember my mom bitching about how cold it was in the restaurant, but Megan said if she turned the heat up, it wouldn't kick in till we were gone so it wasn't worth it. I remember her laughing, and us joking around.

She gave me the biggest hug when I left. She was sad that she couldn't go to my baby shower, but my boyfriend spent the next day with her. When my boyfriend and I got home, I gave them their own baby shower by showing them all the gifts on FaceTime and in person.

This is Megan at the funeral before she was cremated. I was holding her hand, trying to warm her up.

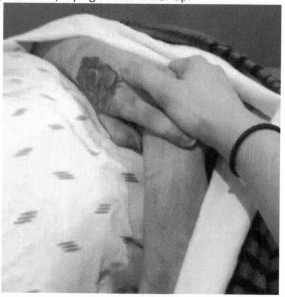

I love you, Megan.

Michele Kelley

Darren Jolly

June 9, 1970 – July 18, 2015

This picture was taken on his birthday 1 month before he died.

$\mathcal{M}$y brother, Darren, is exactly 1 year, 8 months and 1 day older than me.

He was 45 years, 1 month and 9 days old when he died. I am 45, 7 months and 6 days as I write this. I know it's silly, but I often wonder – am I the older one now? How do I classify my existence in my family – am I an only child? I am officially older than my older brother ever was.

My brother had a headache. To be more specific, a migraine that he had for days. He got migraines often and they were usually quite bad, this time being no different. On Thursday, he posted a comment on Facebook on how he felt so awful, that his headache just wouldn't let up. I asked if he needed anything and we talked about how I would bring him over some pain relief the next day.

On Friday, as promised, I stopped by his house. I didn't stay long as he still wasn't feeling well. I told him I loved him, gave him a hug and left.

He went to bed that night and never woke up.

I, myself, woke up from a dream around 3:30-4:00 AM. I was agitated and uneasy, and I didn't know why. Eventually, I fell back asleep and the next morning I got up and ready for the day. We were going fishing, and, on our way, I received a message that Darren was unresponsive, and a family member was needed right away. I wasn't given any more information, but I knew deep down that something was terribly wrong.

When I got to his house, there was an ambulance out front— no lights on. No sirens. A police officer was standing there waiting for me. He didn't have to say the words, he just looked at me and gently shook his head. The officer asked me to go in the house, so I could identify Darren's body. I opened the front door, walked up the stairs, and my brother, whom I just hugged in the very same spot only the afternoon before, was laying there in an unzipped body bag with an intubation tube still in his mouth.

That was the end.

This is the beginning.

My brother and I grew up in a small town and, being so close in age, we knew each other's friends well. We often were seen at the same events, associating with the same crowd. We always knew what the other was up to and we were very close.

Throughout the years, we lived in different cities but never stopped talking.

Darren was my person.

My confidant.

The one person I could always count on no matter what.... I could call him and vent about a bad day. I could ask for his help with something, it didn't matter, he was always there for me.

He lived with me for a while shortly after my daughter was born, and we spent many nights hanging out together at Chapters (a book store); he went one way, I went another and we browsed through the books and just chilled out.

Darren was a welder by trade, an incredible artist; he painted an amazing Disney themed mural on my daughter's bedroom wall, and he had a passion for drawing NASCAR and superheroes. He took his artistic skill to a new level when he became a tattoo artist. He changed people's lives with his artwork, and thousands of people now have a piece of him on them forever, and his amazing skill will never be forgotten.

We had a lot of fun memories; like him handing out porridge for Halloween because he ran out of candy. It was a typical Darren move. He was funny, loving, kind and a special individual.

It has been two years, and I still can't figure out how I will live without him.

His light was put out because of a headache.

Never in a million years would I have ever thought my brother would have died from a headache.

I love you, I miss you and you will always be in my heart.

Sheri Jolly

This picture was taken October 15, 2011

He was comforting my daughter Emily. She was sad because no one was playing with her. (He was tattooing her footprints on my foot).

How was I supposed to breathe life into something no longer living?
When you were so dead inside it seemed all your oxygen was missing.
You were filled with such an emptiness that was beyond what I could comprehend,
And slowly started filling your body with destruction only trying to help yourself mend.
Over time your drug of choice began spiraling out of control,
And what was once thought to be a resolution began to gradually destroy your soul.
You were lost in a sea of turmoil and chaos with not knowing where to turn,
And sought help that got you nowhere; for true help, you did yearn.

I should have been that for you but instead, I stood by and watched,
And like so many other things in life this too I have botched.
I will always remember the last time I saw you and forever mourn,
I left you there knowing that you were broken, and you were torn.
There is so much with you I wish I would have done differently,
I wish I knew back then my mistakes would cause this type of severity.
You are precious to me and I will carry you in my heart,
We are no longer together physically but spiritually will never be apart.

So what is it that we can do with these people who are so lost?
For those who throw away everything not fully understanding the cost.

So many options yet not knowing the right one to make;
Tough love, rehab, jail, counseling, tell me which one it will take.
Some will get all and some will have none of these choices.
Some will be listened to and some will remain without voices.
What works for one won't work for the next and some will remain the same,
So how do we know what to do when we don't even know how to play this game?
There are so many things unknown in a situation such as this,
So much time will pass and there will be so many things you miss.
In reality, you cannot force a person to make a certain decision,
Just like you cannot stop them from running straight into a collision.
What you can do is never let your hope fade or bury your love deep inside,
Their choices are not about you do not make this about your pride.
Set boundaries as needed but give them unconditional love,
Do not hate, discriminate, or slander we have to learn to rise above.
In an instant their lives can be gone, they'll no longer be in sight,
Pray to God for them constantly for this could be their last night.

In Memory of Savanna Carol Knight
09/09/1986-05/15/2017.

I Knew You

People seem to be blinded, even with their sight.
In reality, they're in the dark, but think they're in the light.
Their vision is blurred; they only see what's on the outside.
With no education their advice they think I should abide.
Those people call you an addict, a druggie, and a dope head.
They tell themselves it's your fault; you are why you're dead.
When one learns drugs are involved they automatically know best.
They have heard this same story before and say you're just like the rest.
How do we show them different? How do we undeceive?
For they didn't know the real you that was hidden underneath.
The drugs destroyed your mind, but never touched your heart.
They do not know your struggles or how life had torn you apart.
No one can ever take away the beauty that I know was in you.
For their opinions for their thoughts can never change what's true.
We all have our faults some just show more than others.
Most of society just keeps theirs hidden under the covers.
I knew you. Savanna, you were so much more than your addiction.
All you wanted out of life was a man that loved you and a few children.
You had so much hurt from things that happened in the past.
So many broken relationships for none of them would last.
And with all of that turmoil, you would still help those in need.
I never had to beg you. I never had to plead.

You were a fighter, Savanna, and I believe that you did your best.
Don't worry what others are saying, just lay your head down and rest.

By Melissa Robinson

(All five of us)

$\mathcal{S}$ometimes it's hard to remember that place before everything began to fall apart.

Our world was ordinary, until it wasn't. We knew about love and laughter and the happiness that surrounds a small-town family, until we didn't.

There were five of us children, and Keven was the youngest. He was funny, smart, handsome, generous and loving. He was a great cook and sometimes talked of going to culinary school. He loved his family (especially his nieces and nephews), the Dallas Cowboys, the Detroit Red Wings, Howard Stern, Andrew Dice

Clay and David Letterman. He was all of these things but what ended up defining his life was that he was an alcoholic.

Like most people who drink, he began in high school, but unlike most of us, the alcohol took hold of him and held on until it took over his life. He lost everything several times over and tried numerous times to get sober. There were at least five stays in rehab both here in Michigan and in Texas that helped only for a short time, but then the bottle would whisper in his ear again and he would get sucked back into the hole. I remember a span of a few months when he was sober and had finally gotten his own apartment. He had furnished it and we went to see him, and he was so very proud of what he had accomplished. And then, once again, it was gone.

As a baby, Keven had very fine blond hair that stood up straight on his head. His first real word was "birdie" and he never crawled he just did a modified army crawl until he started walking. As a small child he got what we now know were horrible migraines which would make him vomit and imprison him in a dark room for a day or two at a time.

He was the most loving guy and the most frustrating guy all at the same time. Our efforts to save him were in vain, but we kept trying. I remember my sister and I taking him to rehab for one of his stays. He had to be there by noon, and by the time we got to him he was drunk. We took him to the facility, but they turned him away and told us to bring him back in 12 hours when he was sober. We did get him checked in finally at midnight that night for a 30 day stay. Seeing him sober and "himself" was like the sun turning back on after a thousand nights of darkness. Unfortunately, that stay ended. He came home, and within a few short weeks we were back where we started. Eventually, his life was taken over by health, and legal and financial issues because of his alcoholism.

On January 30, 2002, Detroit (along with much of the Midwest) was hit with a massive ice storm—the power was out for several days. I was an associate manager at a retail store and was at work, despite the power outage. When I got home (before the days when we all had cell phones) I had a hysterical message from my niece to get to the hospital. My beautiful baby brother had attempted to hang himself in my mom's basement. He was on life support for two days, and after multiple tests, we were told that he was brain dead.

On February 2, 2002 we made the decision to pull his life support. It was a devastating day. He was only 37 years old.

That day, our family became a little bit smaller. The world became a little bit darker. But for Keven, the pain was over. He is still alive in our hearts and minds and, through us, he lives on.

(Our Keven)

Wendy Richardson

Donna and Diane
Twinkies Forever

Dear Diane,

$\mathcal{I}$ cannot recall exactly the last time I saw your face or our exact conversation. As much as that was part of my grief at first, I now realize that was a blessing in disguise, because I would be trying to analyze every word, movement and see if I would have known you would be leaving soon.

The reason I can't remember is because we talked so often, and about everything and nothing, that I guess remembering the exact last conversation doesn't matter. We had silly conversations most of the time.

Many times, we laughed and laughed at the dumb things we did that drove Mom and Dad crazy. Like the time we were about fifteen or so and drove the car through the garage door! I had told you not to put your foot on the accelerator. Or the time that we got tipsy and the car got a flat, and we both got out of the car on a patch of ice, slipping around and decided to call Mom to send Dad out at midnight to rescue us. While talking to mom, we got the giggles. She was so mad at us, which made us laugh even harder into the phone. She didn't say a word when we walked in though, which made it even funnier to us.

Every time we were in trouble, we would laugh, which made them think we were crazy.

We were.

I still bring it up to Mom, and you know what? I start laughing, and she still gets that look of anger on her face, and it still makes me laugh even harder. You have to be enjoying that!

Why Mom and Dad didn't kill us is still a mystery to me.

You were the one who I knew had my back as we got older and cared about me more than anyone else, and it went likewise. Life brought us through so many struggles, but nothing could have prepared me when you left.

Dad died five weeks after I was married, and that was tough. But on August the 13th, 2015, you were gone, and that was the most devastating thing that I have ever experienced.

I still feel the pain and anguish as I have lived through Hell in the real sense. I didn't think I would make it at first, but then on a special Good Friday, someone prayed over me, and three red cardinals came flying toward me as I was backing into the garage. They looked as if they'd go through my windshield. I asked out loud if it was you, Dad and Grandma. A cloud of pain seemed to lift from me little-by-little after that. And gradually, I knew I would make it. Life started coming back to me. And someone whispered to me that you were always taking care of your nieces, Katie and Loren, whom you loved and adored. I heard you laugh when something happens, or when I'm with my first-grade class. I hear you lament for me when I'm sad.

The first solo birthday was terrifying. My co-workers ordered a pizza and a cake as a surprise. I had prayed to have a visit from you that day. Well, the toppings on the pizza were your favorites—not mine. And the red velvet cake, was your favorite again, too. They could never have known. I knew then that you were there.

Diane, you know I started getting healthy again. I now walk daily, mostly at the cemetery from Dad to you and back again. About five-thousand steps. I look for animals to pop out at me, and I believe that somehow you are there. I walk for you who can no longer walk with me, or maybe you do.

I love you forever, my twin,

Your fellow Twinkie,

Donna

Below is the letter I left in here coffin, with a box of Twinkies as that is what we were called.

Dearest Diane,

So... You haven't called me for several days now. I'm going through withdrawals.

I'm not sure how I'm supposed to survive life without you now; we were together from before birth.

I can't imagine being only one half of a twin. Birthdays will never be the same. Parties never the same. Nothing will ever be the same.

I have been remembering all the "Double Trouble" things we did that drove Mom and Dad crazy.

We did have fun.

I will miss you, and I hope you will be waiting for me. Do not leave me alone. You were the one whom I know cared for me the most, called me the most, and wanted to know how my day was.

I will miss you more than anyone can imagine.

I love you,

Your Twin, "Twinkie"

Donna

To Where You Are

By Josh Groban
Who can say for certain
Maybe you're still here
I feel you all around me
Your memory's so clear
Deep in the stillness
I can hear you speak
You're still an inspiration
Can it be
That you are my forever love
And you are watching over me
From up above
Fly me up to where you are
Beyond the distant star
I wish upon tonight
To see you smile
If only for a while to know you're there
A breath aways not far to where you are
Lie gently sleeping
Here inside my dream
And isn't faith believing
All power can't be seen
As my heart holds you
Just one beat away
I cherish all you gave me
Everyday
Cause you are my forever love
Watching me from up above
And I believe that angels breathe
And that love will live on

And never leave
Fly me up to where you are
Beyond the distant star
I wish upon tonight
To see you smile
If only for a while to know you're there
A breath aways not far to where you are
I know you're there
A breath aways not far to where you are

My brother, Adrian

When I heard about this project, I was immediately excited. Then, when sitting down to write about my brother, I got stumped. It began to almost feel as though I was rewriting his eulogy all over again. My amazing, incredibly smart, sarcastic, big brother has been gone for just over sixteen years.

Since 2001.

That's right, the same year that was quite possibly the worst year for so many other peoples' lives, also turned out to be the worst for my family as well.

I, however have a different reason for hating September, and that's because Adrian's birthday was in September. And now, writing this in September around his birthday, I feel so connected to him, missing him more than ever.

My brother and I have a unique story. We were adopted and from separate families, so absolutely no blood ties. He was five-and-a-half-years older than I, and so wise.

Wise beyond his years.

He'd joke with me about trying to be cool and how much I thought it would matter later in my life. Truth be told, I knew he was right, but I'd never admit that to him.

Growing up, I envied him. I envied everything he was able to do and how well he was able to do it. I was the social one, he was the smart—cure cancer type of smart—one.

He always had a plan and always had a backup, just in case.

We argued as most brother/sister combos do and always knew that we loved each other.

Growing up, I understood that he had medical issues; the same ones my mom had. He happened to have the same medical genetic condition our Mom had, but didn't want to pass on to her children, as it's a rare one that gives a shorter-than-normal life span, which was why she had chosen adoption.

I don't think I ever fully understood what his limitations and concerns were. That is, until he went to work one day, and had to be taken to the hospital.

He had heart-attack-like pain and symptoms. He was rushed to surgery to repair his heart. A surgery that was only supposed to last a few hours turned into a marathon surgery. One that gave him back to us. His valves had torn and, when the surgeon went in to repair them, they found his ascending aorta (the largest vein in our bodies) was dangerously thin—so thin that the surgeon had described it as wet tissue paper. Had my brother sneezed or coughed before surgery, his aorta would have ruptured, and he would have never made it out. This surgery opened my naive eyes, telling me that I could actually lose my brother. Heck, we almost lost him on the table and in the hospital. That surgery was three years before he died.

The coming years were spent with laughter and plans. Plans of broadening my horizons and his as well. He was in an accelerated college degree program, one that allowed him to study abroad. After picking up French within weeks of taking his high school classes, he had fallen in love with the culture, language, allure and desire to be in France. Like I said, he was so smart. His talents took him so far and were just starting to round out and finish up for the beginning of the rest of his life.

In March of that year, I went for a visit. One with my high school class, and that would allow me to step away and go visit him. Those few short days I had with him were amazing. I forgot to take pictures of my time with him. *The last time I saw him alive.* I still cannot believe I didn't take any. But we laughed, he cooked, we drank. I was amazed at the man he had become. A completely different person from what I remembered. He had become someone who was discovering himself and what he wanted from life in a different country and emerging as an even wiser person.

When I left, I had to hop on a train to take us to the last leg of the trip, one that I was supposed to see him before I went, but he got held up and I didn't get to say the actual final good bye. The problem with those types of moments are that you never think they will be your last.

I should have missed that train to give him one final goodbye hug.

One final *I love you*.

I could have given him the rest of my French currency. He needed a haircut. I should have just figured out what to do later and miss the train

If only I had known.

The next few months were a blur as I was preparing for my end of the year finals and ready to become a senior and graduate. I had so much "more important" things to think about. We had weekly Sunday calls, and I'd usually hop on for a bit and that would be that. He'd lecture me about needing to brush up more on my French if I was planning to live with him for a year as I needed to know the language. And I'd banter back with how I wouldn't need to because I'd have him as my tour guide.

The morning we got the phone call was just like any other. I had a landline phone right by my bed and usually the calls were for me and, without thinking, at 6:33 in the morning I tiredly answered the ringing phone. And all I could think was "Why is someone calling so early and during my precious summer vacation?" I'd heard the woman's voice before, but still didn't understand why she was calling. It was the president of the student ambassador program that he was in. I walked over to the stairs to holler at my mom, who was getting ready for work, that she had a call. I shut off my phone and began to shuffle back to bed, when I heard a gut-wrenching scream, followed by a thud.

I rushed up the stairs to my mother who had collapsed. She just kept repeating, "He's dead! Adrian's dead. My baby is gone."

The next few days were of us making arrangements to fly over to France and claim him and his belongings.

When we arrived, there was so much to do. The school had organized a wake, a ceremony and for his friends to meet with us. We had the most heartwarming reception I could have ever imagined. We were told stories of the man he was away at college in a foreign country. The fact that my brother spoke better French than some natural born Frenchmen do. How he was so kind and welcoming to everyone he had met.

The stories kept coming.

They put together a book for us to have that had stories and memories from so many people: teachers, students, friends and coworkers. They all had written in it. There were pictures and great stories. I, still, to this day love that book. We were awarded

130

with some medals and a gorgeous marble plaque (it has a twin) that still is at the university. I knew how well he had touched my life, but to read it so many times over and over again from these people, made those weeks there more bearable.

He was my big brother; my voice of reason. My best friend.

I have done a lot of healing in the last years. I have discovered and realized how much of me has changed. I have discovered how proud of myself he would be. And on the days that are particularly hard, I listen to a song that instantly makes me think of him, and I know that's his way of saying, "You've got this!"

Sometimes, we forget how much the pain hides. We forget to remember the memories we do have and not the ones we will never make. I am still hurt over the fact that I will never become a sister-in-law, an aunt, or have nieces and nephews. I hurt for the uncle my children will never meet. And I have learned that it's okay to be hurt by those things. It's okay for me to be angry. It's okay to relive and remember him. It's okay to feel the pain all over again.

Chelsey and Adrian

Chelsey Davis

Me (Beth Anne) and my sister, Amanda Boucher

*T*he first time I saw you was in the hospital. I told everyone that I was three years and three months older. I was so proud to be an older sister, and I couldn't believe I was once as small as you! Most days, I could be seen pulling you around the house in a laundry basket. I didn't like sharing our parents' attention, but I was fascinated by you.

The first time I saw you as my best friend was when we were children. You were my constant companion and, throughout most of our lives, we were inseparable. We had active imaginations and traveled the world through our creations. One day we were Cinderellas, stuck doing chores and waiting for our Prince Charmings. The next I was the teacher, and you were my diligent pupil. After that, we would be transported to a castle and we would dance at an extravagant ball.

Every day was an adventure with you.

The first time I saw you as more than my sister was when you became a mother. When your children were born, you and I both had tears in our eyes. I've never seen you more in love with another human being. You were always selfless and compassionate, and motherhood only intensified those qualities. Your world revolved around your two daughters and they filled you with such joy.

The last time I saw you happy was on our road trip to the hospital. We were worried about Mom and didn't want to be in a car for three hours, but we made the best of it, even if you did spill an entire bag of pretzels on the floor and on the front seat of my car. We laughed, talked about ridiculous things, and sang at the top of our lungs. I still haven't been able to bring myself to listen to the CDs we listened to on that trip.

The last time I saw you alive was two weeks before your death. We had spent a week together in close quarters visiting mom in ICU and started fighting about something stupid. We were getting on each other's nerves easily and couldn't wait to go back to our separate homes, states apart.

Until this week, for years, we had spent every night talking on the phone. The last time I saw you alive I walked away from you instead of saying goodbye.

The last time I saw you was at the funeral home. You were lying on a table in the chapel. It had only been a few days after you died, but you didn't look like yourself. I was the last to go in, and I felt like I couldn't breathe. I wasn't able to say anything that I needed to say. That day was one of the hardest days of my life.

Beth Anne Roe

My brother, Jake, and me (Katie)

It was an exceptionally cold few days in February, and we hadn't seen each other since Christmas. I was back home from out of state for a few days to see you and do some planning. We went to Bdubs for dinner that night, and I remember you so vividly, sitting across from me and smiling from ear-to-ear as I showed you my ring. I was so excited to tell you all the plans for my wedding and how excited I was for you to be a part of my big day. So excited that I forgot to ask how *you* were doing.

I slowed down my speech and focused on you, finally asking you how you were. And in typical Jake style, you tipped your head back, covered your mouth and let out a deep laugh. This was your go to when you wanted to make me feel like everything was going well and you were doing alright.

You smiled and said you couldn't be happier. You told me about your plans to get your own place and start volunteering, and you seemed genuinely happy.

The next couple of days I had planned to go to a few bridal stores and then to a big wedding expo in the cities (we lived in MN so yes, the cities are plural haha). I asked you to go, fully anticipating you to think it was lame and want to go out with your friends instead, but you wanted to join in and help out.

The first store we walked into was all fancy and glittery and made, even me, feel uncomfortable. I looked back at you, standing with Dad, looking at veils up front. I thought for sure you would be thinking by now "Why did I agree to this!?" But you just stood there with a smile on your face as if you were telling me from across the room that you were proud of me.

From there we went to a few more stores then headed for home. The next day was the bridal expo, and I think I hooked you into saying you'd go by telling you there was going to be free samples of cake. We got ready for the day, and the *Weather Channel* kept saying that there was a blizzard coming and that the weather was only going to get worse later on in the day. You had to work the next day, and lived an hour south of Mom and Dad, where the roads were a lot more treacherous. I was scheduled to fly back home the next day, so neither of us wanted to lose the time together. I said I would skip the expo and you said you weren't worried about the roads. But as the weather got worse, Mom and Dad stepped in, and we all decided it was safer for you to head out then before the storm hit.

You encouraged me to go to the expo because the weather wasn't hitting as hard in the cities. I gave you a big hug and said I couldn't wait to come back home in a few months and plan some more. You smiled and headed down to your bedroom to pack. I didn't like leaving you like this and something in my stomach said to tell you I loved you, so before Mom, Dad and I took off, I stood at the top of the basement steps and yelled, "I love you, bud!"

and you yelled back up, "Love you, Teek". (A childhood nickname that only my Dad and Jake call/called me) Those were the last words I would ever hear from you. We talked since then, but only via text and Facebook.

Skip ahead to that dreadful day… April 25, 2013, 4:13am and my fiancée, David's phone went off. We both sat up in bed. David answered the phone and kept saying "Yes I am with her, over and over. I tried to prepare myself, as I knew my grandfather had been sick and knew phone calls that brought bad news often started like this. But something was different. Why was my father repeatedly asking if David was with me? David handed me the phone a little confused himself. I will never forget the sound of my father's voice; it was one that I had never heard before, "Kate, Jake's gone. He's gone…"

It started out softly and quivering. I just sat there; I couldn't have prepared for that. I didn't want to believe what I was hearing.

I couldn't believe it.

I finally was able to speak. "What!?" was all I could get out. My dad broke into a million pieces on that phone. He started bawling and said, "I'm sorry, I'm sorry, I'm sorry…"

I lived 800 miles from home, was supposed to work that day and no one was awake to call. My mom got on the phone and said, "We're getting you home, pack a bag".

That morning will forever haunt me.

It's not just birthdays, holidays, and looking at old pictures. It's feeling the rain hit my skin. It's listening to the radio, driving home. It's looking into my daughter's eyes. It's never just sometimes. Jake, I know you're in a better place and that you're probably the happiest you've ever been, and that still doesn't change how much I miss you.

I wish I could invent a word that can encompass the ache, "missing" is too small.

Katie Harmeier

My brother, Rick, and me (Cori) on my wedding day

$\mathcal{M}$y younger brother, Rick, died on June 7, 2013. In the

spring of 2016 I had to write and give a eulogy for my public speaking class. While I did give a eulogy at my brother's service, I chose to use parts of what I originally wrote for my assignment.

What determines a person's longevity? Is it a healthy lifestyle, genetics, or maybe you think that we're here for a reason and once we've completed our purpose our time here is done?

I personally don't know what determines how long we live; but I do know that my brother Rick taught me some important life lessons in the twenty-four years that he was with us.

The first thing I learned from him was unconditional love. He was born exactly seven days after my ninth birthday. I was the first person to feed him in the hospital and in that moment, I loved him already. He taught me how to be a role model by emulating me.

As a toddler, he wanted to wear make-up and carry a purse. He copied my tastes in music and even shared my love of skulls. Now, I'm not a very touchy-feely person by nature, but Rick showed me that it's ok to be affectionate. He always made sure to give everyone goodnight and good-bye hugs and kisses. One time when he was about three or four, I was going somewhere alone with our mother and Rick ran after us with his arms outstretched for a hug saying, "I want to come, too" and making kissing noises. He did want to come, but he also wanted more hugs and kisses.

I learned just how important a sense of humor is. Rick had this sarcastic, dry sense of humor that our whole family really appreciated. If you ever said anything in error, he would raise an eyebrow and smirk... and you just knew that he was going to tease you mercilessly all while laughing with you. The two of us would often team up and tease our mother. One Thanksgiving we were all sitting around the table at my house and our mom was telling us how she likes to keep a little bit of the Christmas spirit all year by keeping one decoration out. Well, instead of saying nutcracker she said nut scratcher! And oh boy did my brother and I have a field day with that one. By the time we were done teasing her everyone's stomachs and faces were sore from laughing so hard. We had a lot of good times together and truly enjoyed each other's company.

We could have fun together doing absolutely anything or nothing at all. This one time when I was a teenager our mom sent us to the grocery store for her; I don't remember what set us off, but we giggled through the entire shopping trip. Once we started laughing we couldn't stop. And that is exactly what hanging out with my brother was like. He could turn the most boring and mundane tasks into something fun and enjoyable. In fact, his friends say the same thing.

Whether you went to a great place like Six Flags with him or just stayed home you would have a blast because Rick made it fun. He showed me what it was to be giving, loyal and empathetic through his everyday actions. He was selfless and was concerned about others. When he saw homeless people he always gave them money, to the point where he wouldn't have anything left for himself. I guess he figured that they needed the money more than he did. If you needed him, he was there for you. He would give anyone a ride regardless of the distance or would literally give the hoodie off his back if someone needed it. He did all of this because he didn't value material things, he valued people and his relationships with them more. He touched so many lives and is greatly loved.

In closing I'd like to end with a quote.

"Your absence has gone through me like a thread through a needle. Everything I do is stitched with its color" –W.S. Merwin

Cori Hass, Richard Vogt's older sister

Kevin Phillip Shober 6/25/1992 - 4/05/2012

Dear Kevin,

At first, every second of every day was spent in anguish with no other possible alternative. Whether neglect on your own part or the driver of the truck that night, the only truth is that you were dead, and my life has never for one second been the same.

Through burning tears, I buried your ashes in the ground while attempting to cling to every minuscule detail of your body, the pitch of your voice, and your infectious laughter we often shared.

I visited those ashes as often as I could in hopes of seeking closure. Countless drawings of water ice (our favorite treat) followed by grief-stricken memories jotted down on scraps of paper were wrapped in plastic baggies and secured in your interchangeable vase atop your grave.

Balloons filled with hope, dreams, and well wishes for your 19th birthday were released to the sky.

Your 21st birthday was celebrated by your side as a few of us gathered to share a beer. Slowly I appreciated that as each birthday and each Holiday arose, I somehow was learning to survive without your physical presence.

Gradually, as my mind grew clearer and my emotions more resilient, I began to accept your death. Although I knew accepting your death meant I would no longer be on equal grieving levels as some of my other bereaved family members, I felt that you would want me to regain my life and happiness even if others could not. As I set forth, I could not help but realize a surge of elation as I slowly started to dissect my grief. As my body healed from the trauma, I began replacing those layers of grief with our fondest memories. Recollections so revered that they will remain solely in my grace.

Now, five years later I am no longer running to retail stores absentmindedly buying an entire rack of clearance items just to soothe my reckless and restless frame of mind. Once the infinite stream of tears subsided, I now look to your photos for comfort and contentment. Although there are somedays when knowing that I will see you again is not enough, I remind myself that I am a fighter and I have survived devastating grief when all odds were against me. I miss your face, I miss your laugh, and I miss you terribly. I continue to keep you alive and by my side through the nineteen years of wonderful memories that I am so grateful to have shared with you.

To reiterate, I love you, baby brother. I miss you. You are forever in my heart.

Love,

Laura

Sara and me (Jeanette)

Dear Sara,

*N*ot a day goes by that I don't think of you.

In two months, it will be the 5th anniversary of you earning your wings. Not a day goes by that this melancholy inside my heart lifts. I have my good days, reflecting on times we've had together. For instance, the holidays are approaching. I often reflect on Halloween—of us Trick-or-Treating while watching horror movies. Then comes Thanksgiving, where you make stuffing (Mom still has your recipe in the kitchen). Lastly, Christmas comes where we always forget to get stocking stuffers, so we haul ourselves out of bed and run to Duane Reade's at 7:00 AM, while eating holiday cookies that we baked (always in excess).

I promise you I will always keep your memory alive with my son. Aidan not only looks like you but has your personality as well. He will know our traditions and how important family is. I wish we could go back to those days when all we worried about was what cookies to make and if we were going to get the door to give kids their candy.

I've always envied you, you know. I envied how independent and fierce you were. You were always the strong one (even though I was the eldest). I'm sorry I've messed up many times, but I'm trying to be different today. I'm trying to be the woman you were...to be strong inside and out.

I will always love you, sis. Thank you for making me appreciate life more. I can't wait until we meet again.

Love always,

Jeanette

My sister, Dee

$\mathcal{M}$y younger sister, Dee, found out in April of 2016 that she had pancreatic cancer.

She and her husband had just moved to North Carolina from Connecticut. I will never forget the day that they both called me to give me the news. Our lives were changed forever.

My sister and I have always been close, and the only reason I was ok with her moving was because I was going to be moving to the shoreline in CT, so I would have been an hour away anyway. I flew there to help with some of her first chemo treatments. Never had I ever seen my sister so upbeat in my entire life. She was going to do all she could and fight as hard as she knew how to beat the disease and move on with her life. We talked and texted every day.

Her texts to me were always something like "Good morning, sister of mine... how are you doing today?" *Sister of mine* is embedded in my brain and forever in my heart. She came back to CT a few times, and every time she had that same look of defiance...that her life was hers. The last time she was back was for the birth of her grandson, and just seeing her shook my world. I'm not sure if, by this point, she didn't want anyone to know or if she really didn't know herself that she wasn't going to make it. I personally believe that she knew in her heart that she wasn't going to.

We talked and talked the entire time she was here. She never spoke of dying. After that, the texts and phone calls got fewer and fewer. I would text or call her husband to check on her.

One day she didn't answer me for over twelve hours, and I messaged him a million times as I was worried sick. When he called me back, he talked to me for over an hour and without telling me straight out, he let me know that things were getting worse.

The next morning, he called and told me that when he had gotten home the evening before, my sister was very incoherent. She was taken to the hospital then for dehydration, and they were running tests. Of course, I wanted to go and be with her, but they always told me to wait to see what the Dr. said. Within the next few days, I found out that my sister was going to be in hospice.

Hospice.

How could this be? She was only 54. She had way too many things left to do.

I left home right away and showed up at my sister's home, the same sister who had always been so put together and so with it. Ironically, the hospice people were there and were trying to tell us what to do and what to expect. My sister got up and left the room many times. She could walk and talk as if things were completely normal. As if she was normal.

I just couldn't wrap myself around the fact that the person in front of me was going to die.

For three weeks my sister was still my sister. I would sit with her and talk and, never ever did I see the look of why me? I, on the other hand, broke down several times during our chats. She would just touch my hand and I would turn away for a minute. I asked her once how she was able to do it. How she could get by knowing that she was going to die soon. Her face never changed a bit when she told me she had accepted it. She told me she had a good life. She said she had a wonderful husband, a wonderful family and had had a wonderful job.

Every night I went to bed, barely sleeping because I just couldn't understand how she could be so calm. She complained here and there about her backaches, if there was too much noise, but nothing else.

She walked up the stairs to her bedroom by herself almost every night until she started needing help as she was losing her strength. I used to try and make her eat all day long. She would pretend she ate or drank what I gave her just to make me feel better.

We laughed...we joked...she called me a warden a few times. What I would give to have that back again you have no idea. My entire family came to see her, too; some from CT, my daughter from CA, some from Florida, some from GA and my uncle and aunt from New Hampshire. One of her sons had lived there for a few years, and the other and his family were staying in the house the same time I was. My dad, who was 80, had dementia and I wasn't even sure if he knew who she was. On the last night they were there he said very loudly how old my sister looked. When I

went upstairs to lay down with my sister as I did most nights, she was crying and saying how she hated that he said that, yet she knew it really wasn't him saying it. I found out later that it was that night that she told her husband that she couldn't do it anymore.

The next night, when almost everyone had left, my daughter and I were sleeping downstairs and my brother-in-law came running in and told us my sister was in so much pain and that she was screaming. I ran up to her. She was sitting up in bed, saying that everything in her body hurt. I called the hospice people who told us to give her some Tylenol and a small dosage of morphine. (Up until that point, she was not taking many drugs at all.) All of the sudden, I had a panic attack. Something I had never had before in my life. I ran into her bathroom and vomited for a few minutes, telling myself to get it together. That this was not about me. It was about Dee!

After that, I spent pretty much every second I could with her. I rubbed her body. Talked to her. I tried to tell her everything was going to be ok. The nurse finally showed up, and she told us to up her morphine a little and, then later in the hallway, told me that this was the beginning of the end and that we just needed to keep her comfortable and, in time, her body would just shut down. I listened to her half-heartedly as she told me that within a few weeks she would be gone. I spent the rest of the night in a chair beside her bed while her husband was next to her. When he left to do something, I would climb right in bed with her and be right by her side. I never stopped touching, rubbing, and

 talking to her as I needed her to know that I was there for whatever she needed. Morning came, and we called the nurse again. Dee just couldn't get comfortable and now seemed to always be agitated. It was time to get her a hospital bed.

What an adventure that was! They came and set up the bed downstairs in their bonus room. I made sure everything she would need was in there for her. I never even wondered how they were going to get her downstairs. Within twenty minutes, four firefighters were up in her room with a dining room chair that they eased her into and got her downstairs into the hospital bed. I did have to leave and go outside because I could hear her screaming, and it was breaking my heart.

The nurse upped her morphine and other medicine then. (I can't remember what it was, but it was like a sleeping pill.) My sister was finally breathing much better, and I could no longer see that line of pain on her forehead. The nurse gave me, my brother- in-law and her two sons instructions on how to administer everything. Once she left, we tried keeping things together and decided that we needed to take turns as we hadn't slept in a while. I was the one who gave her most of the medicine, so I went to sleep first. I slept for three hours and came back down and could tell she was still resting comfortably. I gave her more medicine and pulled up a chair and rubbed her head, and her tiny arms and kept talking to her, telling her it was ok. I told her how much I loved her and how horribly I was going to miss her. I kept telling her how much her family loved her and loved how she kept us all together and how she was the heart of our family. Around 2 AM as I was talking and stroking her hair, my sister opened her eyes, closed them and took a breath of sorts, spit things out of her mouth and was gone...

She was gone so fast that all I could do was scream for the others. I wasn't leaving her side if there was a chance she was still there. My poor brother-in-law was beside himself because he was half awake and was just about to come downstairs when he heard me scream for them.

She was gone.

The nurse came then, and my brother-in-law didn't even know which mortuary to call as he really was not prepared for it.

Soon, he found one, and I stayed in with the nurse and helped her with my sister. I helped take off her nightgown. I helped bathe her. I held her arm as if she was still there and I talked to her while I was helping. I picked out some clothes that she would have liked, and I helped the nurse put those on, too. And then the one last thing I will never ever forget in my life was her being taken out of the house, knowing that she would never return again.

My life was shattered.

The greatest thing about that time was that I will never ever have to regret not being there for and with her. I just can't get rid of this huge hole in my heart.

Diane Rouillard

The Last Time I Saw You

My brother, Eric, and me (Robyn)
November 13, 2005 - my wedding day.

$\mathcal{T}$he last time I saw my brother alive was the day of my wedding.

I arrived at my parents' house that morning around 10:00 a.m. to get dressed in my gown. My parents were up, but my brother was still sleeping. At some point, my father woke him up to get dressed. I knew that he was woken up because I heard him screaming that he did not want to put on his tuxedo and see the so-called "phony" family members. I heard him slam the bathroom door, and I was afraid he was going to throw the tux in the pool. Somehow my father got him dressed.

The limousine arrived, and we all got in. I noticed that my brother had a flask. I held my tongue. I didn't want to get into a screaming match with him. The limousine arrived at the country club. Everyone got out but my brother, he was going to stay behind and be the liaison for picking up relatives. I was busy with the photographer and had not noticed that my brother was not back. The time came for the wedding party group picture.

I looked around, "Where's Eric?"

I was told that he had not arrived back. I thought that was strange as he had been gone for over two hours. Again, I was instructed to get into the center of the photograph.

I blurted, "How can I? Eric isn't here. What, am I going to look back twenty years at this photo, and it will be as if he never existed?"

I shook my head. My husband calmed me and got me to take the shot. We did a few more family photos. Eric's absence was felt, especially in the picture with just my parents. We were a family of four, taking pictures as a family of three seemed awkward. I tried to get my brother on his cell, but he was not picking up. Eric was supposed to walk Baby down the aisle. They were the ring bearers. I refused to go down the aisle without him being present.

Everyone was seated, the sun was about to set, and my dream of walking down the aisle with someone as *sunrise sunset* on the violin was playing was quickly fading away.

Again, I refused to walk down the aisle until Eric was there.

He finally arrived, drunk as a skunk. He could barely stand. The sun had already set. My mother walked me down the aisle as my father had to hold my brother up. During the ceremony, he was swaying and could barely stand. My dad decided it was best for him to sit off to the side.

I tried to get some photographs with my brother right before the reception, but he could barely keep his eyes open. He disappeared for about thirty minutes, and then came back into the hall. He was drunk and probably high. I was pissed at him for ruining the photographs and for being late. I took him outside and started yelling at him. I know I told him that he was selfish and being an asshole, that he could not afford me one day to be a princess and the center of attention. Again, he told me that I should not bend over backward for the "phony" relatives.

The time for speeches came. I knew my brother was going to be giving one. My skin was crawling, as I had no idea what he was going to say. He stood up and then quickly leaned on a chair for support. He roasted me, my husband, and all the family members. He slurred his words and spoke how he felt. The band tried to play him off several times, but he did not have it. Rather than talk to him again, I tried to brush it off and ignore him for the rest of the night. I did not even ask him to dance with me. I thought he was a selfish bastard and I wanted nothing to do with him.

The next day was the wedding goodbye brunch. However, my mother turned it into the unveiling of my grandmother's stone. Eric was supposed to be at the cemetery.

He was nowhere in sight.

I thought he would meet us later at the restaurant.

Nope.

I had cooled off and wanted to speak to him about his behavior. Plus, I wanted a decent photograph of my sibling during my wedding weekend.

Over the next few weeks, I left voice mail messages and sent a few e-mails. He finally replied to an e-mail, saying that he was sorry for his behavior at my wedding and he was trying to clean up his act.

I went to my parents' house New Year's Day with my newly adopted greyhound. I wanted Eric to meet Makani. He did not emerge from his room the entire time. My husband made a snide remark that he might be dead. My parents laughed it off. Lee and I were concerned.

A few more weeks went by, and I still haven't seen or spoken to Eric. I got a call that Baby died. Eric loved doing this routine with Baby on the couch getting her to count with her paw. I wanted to speak to him because I wanted to know how he was coping. He still lived in the same house as Baby. My parents had a funeral for Baby, and she was dressed in the outfit she wore at the wedding. Eric was not present at the funeral.

I was still annoyed with him for his behavior the day of my wedding and wanted to speak to him about that. I still wanted a picture with my sibling. I had one from my marriage where I was practically holding him up, his face was beet red, and he looked drunk. I needed and wanted a normal one.

I went to sleep on February 12, 2006. Nothing abnormal had happened that day, other than me begging my parents to set up a trust so I could take care of Eric should something happen to them.

That night, I dreamt of my brother.

I woke up on February 13, 2006 and felt that a part of me was missing. I couldn't understand why I felt so off and why I had a dream with my brother saying goodbye to me. Later that day, I was pulled out of a work meeting. My best friend was on the phone, and she told me that someone was coming to get me at work. I screamed that Eric was dead and I hit the floor. So many emotions went through me. I struggled for many years regarding the comment I made about the wedding party photograph. I looked at that picture once and ripped it up. All I could see was the place where my brother should have stood. I'm grateful that my wedding was shot in prints and not digital.

It's much easier to hide a box of prints than a file on a computer.

I do regret that the last time I had seen my brother was not a positive experience for either of us. It's ironic as weddings are considered a positive milestone. The family that was at the wedding, for the most part, turned their backs on my parents and me. Eric's speech was correct.

Everyone assumed he died from illegal drugs and alcohol.

He did die in his sleep from drugs and alcohol.

However, it was prescription drugs that were prescribed by a psychologist and ethyl from over the counter cough syrup. We found out months later from the medical examiner that he had fetal lobulations of the kidney. His body could not handle the prescription drugs, combined with the cough syrup, and the high fatty foods he consumed that day. It was unclear if his kidneys shut down then as he asphyxiated on vomit or the other way around. It didn't and shouldn't matter.

He was gone. I regret my last comments to him and the wedding guests about him. Most of all, I'm sorry for the bad judgment on him, my parents, and myself from friends, family and society. It shouldn't matter how he died. He was twenty-three.

No one should die in their twenties.

He had his whole life ahead of him.

Robyn Gabe

Robby Wilkins
10/31/1975-8/23/2002

My brother, Robby, and me (Hilary)

*T*he last time I saw you was my wedding weekend in 2001.

I remember picking you up from the airport and you being so happy for me and the man I was about to marry. The night of my rehearsal, when CiCi said a prayer and mentioned those who could not be with us, you came and put your arm around me because you knew I was crying since Papa and Grandma Lucy couldn't be there.

After everything was over, and we were back at Momma's for the night and I had gone to bed. I remember you couldn't sleep, and you came and woke me up like you used to when we were little.

We went outside and sat and talked for a long time. We talked about spending our summers at our Mammy and Papa's when we were little and how much fun we used to have there. We also talked about June, how she and her family pretty much raised us, and how we never wanted to go home when Momma or Daddy would come to pick us up because we hated our home life so much.

We talked about how you used to come lay with me until I fell back asleep if I woke you up because I'd had a bad dream.

We talked about our lives and where they had taken us. It was as if somehow, we knew that that night would be the last time we were together.

The next morning, you came and woke me up and rode with me when Momma dropped me off to get my hair done. I remember at my wedding you and, my soon-to-be-sister-in-law, were quite smitten with each other, thinking how my future mother and father-in-law must have hated that.

We took a few pictures that day, and then you got drunk and chucked a bag of rice at my head when I was leaving. I got so mad at you, but I still left my new husband to go and hug you goodbye before I got in the limo.

Driving away, I turned and looked out the window, and that was the last time I saw you.

We had a couple of phone calls over the next year and four months, but it was never the same as that weekend.

The night you died, I was at a party and my knees gave out when I was walking. I later found out from the investigators that it appeared that you had fallen on your knees when you died.

I fully believe I felt it. I miss you, Robby.

Hilary Wilkins

Nicholas Aaron Arthur
7/7/81-11/5/12

Me (Nicole) and Nicholas, my brother

$\mathcal{K}$ind, lovable, huggable, always smiling. Those are words people use to describe my "Baby Brudder." Wait, I'm getting ahead of myself. First, let me tell you about him.

Nicholas was born in July of 1981; he was eighteen months younger than me. Growing up, he and I were close. We fought like normal brothers and sisters, kicking each other under the kitchen table, he's touching me in the car, or the occasional *get out of my room!* As we grew older and had our own lives, we weren't as close as we once were. But, we were always there for each other and we always knew that we could count on each other.

When we were teenagers, as many teenagers do, my brother started experimenting with drinking, drugs and partying. When I turned nineteen, I had my son and I entered "real adulthood." As Nicholas entered his early twenties, he continued to party and live life free of responsibilities.

In 2007 at the age of 26, Nicholas' first child (his daughter) was born. He was a beaming, proud father, ready to change his life and give his daughter everything she wanted. Sadly, the world had its grip and Nicholas tried to change. But, he remained enamored by all the fun and partying. 2 ½ years later, in 2010, Nicholas' second child (his son) was born. Nicholas was again a proud father, with a son to call his own, and ready to show him all the world had to offer.

At that point in Nicholas' life, his drug abuse had become severe. I was naïve to how bad the abuse had become. I only knew when he did come around he was high and annoying, and I didn't want to be around him. In fall of 2012, my niece was a midget league cheerleader. We spent our Sundays at the local football field, without my brother. But, the end of the season came, and Nicholas decided to come to a game. Although it was fall, for some reason it was hot that Sunday. I couldn't wait until the game was over to get out of that field and into the car for some air conditioning. When the game was finishing up, my son and I hurried out of the field to the car, trying to beat the crowd.

I heard someone behind me calling out. "Hey! Hey! Sis!"

But, we keep walking to the car. As my son and I sat in the car, my brother caught up and said, "Are you not even gonna give me a hug?" He bent over, gave me a big squeeze and said, "I love you, Sis."

As I put my arms around Nicholas to hug him, I could feel his frail body. My fingers rubbed against his ribs, and then his spine as I hugged him. I couldn't help but think how skinny he felt. As I took a long, deep breath I smelled his cologne and said, "I love you, too".

Then Nicholas opened the back door to give my son a hug and said "I love you, Bubba. Bye." Then, Nicholas closed the door, turned and walked away.

Those were the last few moments that I spent with my brother while he was alive on this earth.

In my mind sometimes, these few moments lasted a lot longer. Unfortunately, a short time later on November 5, 2012, around 10am, I received a call from my grandma. I remember every word and thinking of the call still causes a chill through my body.

Nan: Nicole, are you sitting down?

Me: I'm laying down

Nan: Nick's gone

Me: What do you mean, he's gone?

Nan: He's dead; they found him against a concrete barrier.

Me: I'll be there in a minute.

At that point, my body and mind was numb; in shock. I was thinking that I was the strong one in the family. *I have to hurry and get dressed and get to my Nan and Pawpaw's. Wait, I have to call my husband. What do I tell him? Nick's dead? No.... I'm dreaming. I heard it wrong. No! No! God no! Please, God no!* My screams were no longer in my head and were now coming loudly from my mouth. I calmed myself enough to call my husband.

He left work, picked me up and went to my grandparents' house. *But, wait! This must be a mistake. Why are people messaging me on Facebook and texting me, wanting to know what happened? How do they know? We don't even know if this is true yet. I have to call the sheriff. They could have made a mistake!* When I called the sheriff's office, I was transferred to the lead detective. The detectives asked for identifiable markings on my brother such as birthmarks, tattoos...tattoos...?

I couldn't remember where they were. I couldn't remember what they were. I had to call my mom to find out.

He had a panther (our high school mascot) on his upper arm. I called the detective back and gave him the info. He said that he'd have to call me back after he checked. About thirty minutes went by, and I couldn't wait any longer. I called the detective and when I asked, I heard him say, "It has now been confirmed by

Kanawha County Sheriff that the body found at the park and ride is that of Nicholas A****, 31 of ****."

I said, "Ok, thank you," then hung up the phone.

Oh God! Now I have to notify my dad who lives out of state. How do I call and tell him on the phone that his child, his only son is gone? Wait! His friend works with him! I'll tell her! So, after calling and letting her know, thankfully she was able to tell him privately and drive him home. By the time my dad arrived, the story of Nicholas was on every local news channel at every airing during the day.

But, we still didn't believe it.

Someone else could have had a tattoo like that.

So, we called the funeral home and they let us know that they haven't received the body yet. There had to be an autopsy. Once we found out that they had received the body, we called and insisted on seeing it. We had to prove that it wasn't Nicholas.

The funeral director warned us that it would be traumatic, and we should wait until they prepped the body. But, we couldn't because it might not be him. So finally, he agrees to let myself, my dad, mom and her husband and my brother's wife to come and view the body. Again, he warned us.

As we're walking down the long hall at the funeral home, my mom and dad were in front. I saw the color drain from my dad's face and I saw the tears implode from their faces.

It must be him.

I got into the room. There was a silver gurney, the kind you see body's laying on, on TV crime shows. Then, I saw the sheet, draping a body, a tall body.

Wait! I see the face!

My heart dropped, I couldn't breathe. *Oh God! It's him! It's real! No! I have to touch him, I'm dreaming. Why is he cold? No! No! No!! It's real! It's him.* The Baby Brudder I protected and loved and fought and teased was lying there lifeless.

He was gone.

The next few days were kind of blurry. I remember being asked to write his obituary, and I did. I made posters of old and new pictures to show a life of love and family and friendship. *But, what happened? How could this happen? Why would God take him?* We still don't know the full events of the night of my brother's death. However, we do know that he was at a known drug dealer's home and his body was found the next morning against a concrete barrier at a local park and ride. We have so many unanswered questions.

Who was Nicholas with?

How did he get to the park and ride?

Did they know he was overdosing and leave him there alone to die?

The autopsy showed that my brother overdosed on Klonopin and Opana. When we were cleaning my brother's room afterwards, we found a paper. Written on the paper was the name of a local rehab, with a phone number and a counselor's name and in big letters it also said GET HELP NOW!

My Baby Brudder wanted help; he needed help, and he didn't get it.

The loss I feel from losing my brother is so deep it's indescribable. Nothing fills the hole in my heart, the void in my life. But, one of my favorite things is almost anyone that knew my brother said he always met them with a smile and a hug. But, sometimes I wonder if I'll forget his smile, or the smell of his cologne, or the final hug. What if I forget what his voice sounded like? I'm thankful to know that the last time Nicholas and I saw each other that I know, without a doubt, we said I love you, and we knew we both meant it.

Nicholas Aaron Arthur
1/2/81 to 11/5/12

Nicole Sovine

My brother, David

*I*n 2011 my brother David was killed at the age of 26, when he was knocked off his bike by a drunk driver. He was my best friend.

Losing him has changed everything.

Dear David,

You were always an important part of my life. I was often jealous of you, and how you charmed everyone you met, and negotiated social situations with ease. When we were together, you introduced me to your friends as if I was not an embarrassment to you. You celebrated my successes, even if they didn't appear to be big achievements to others, because you understood how difficult it had been for me to get there. I grew up not understanding why I was different. When finally, my autism diagnosis explained everything for me, you understood that this was not the bad news some people thought it was. You celebrated this new understanding with me and offered nothing but support.

At times I felt somewhat distanced from other family members, who grieved so differently to me. They found comfort in being together and talking about their feelings, whereas I found this sometimes stressful for my autistic brain. I really needed time alone to process my thoughts. I didn't take an extended time off work because I found comfort in keeping up my usual activities and routines. I tried to keep up my usual mealtimes, bedtimes and hobbies, because they gave me some normality in a very abnormal situation.

At times, people seemed concerned that I was not resting enough or grieving "correctly," and seemed to feel that if I did not cry in group situations, that one day I would explode. But that did not happen. Grieving in my own way has turned out to be the best thing for me, and you gave me the strength to know that I am allowed to do things differently if I need to.

I was surprised to learn you had told all your friends that I was planning to go to university in my 30s. I knew you showed encouragement to me, but I had no idea you really felt that way inside enough to tell other people how excited you were for me. I considered delaying. After all, you had only just died, and I wasn't sure if it was appropriate to start something for myself after something so sad. But then I thought about your excitement for me, and I decided that going to university would bring me happiness, so I wrote my application, without the help you had promised me, and I sent it off, and I was offered a place.

I missed you so much once the courses started. I was at an age when most people would have been much better equipped to negotiate the challenges. It was not easy for me to manage the courses, and when I came across difficulties, I felt a huge sense of emptiness that you were not there to talk to, as I knew you would have suggestions and encouragement to offer.

It has been difficult to find positivity after something so sad. At first, it was so utterly shocking to lose you, and it still has not fully sunk in that you are really gone. Eventually, I started to want happiness in life. I didn't want to always feel sad, and I didn't think you would want that for me either. I realised that good things would not just happen to me while I sat there waiting; I had to make my own good in life.

In 2013, I heard about a road safety campaign called *Safe Drive Stay Alive*. Every year they do live shows at a theatre, and invite students from local schools, colleges and youth groups. There are speakers from the emergency services, people who have been in road accidents, or who have lost family members. It sounded like a powerful campaign that had a real impact on new drivers. I think you would have been impressed by it.

I wanted to be involved.

I found contact details, but I was nervous about getting in touch, what to say, and what they would think of me. But I thought of you and the encouraging things you would say, and I found the strength to make the first approach. I had an initial meeting with the person who oversees the event, and it was nice to hear more about it, but I was worried about how they would perceive me. *Would they think I was too shy to be capable of public speaking?* Although holding a conversation could be challenging and nerve-wracking, in some ways public speaking was easier for me, as there were no worries about predicting what the other person would say, as they would just listen, so I could plan in advance what I would say and seek other opinions about whether it was right.

In November 2014, I participated as a volunteer speaker. I stood on the stage and spoke to audiences of 800 teenagers about how it felt to lose you, my brother, in a road accident. It was terrifying, but so, *so* worthwhile. I hope that by doing it, fewer people will die like you did, and fewer families will have to suffer a loss like ours, and yours.

I still participate every year. I have met other people who have lost loved ones in a similar way, and I feel less alone in my loss. It has given me perspective, and a means of doing something positive. I wish you could see me, David. I think you would tell me, in that calm, understated way that always meant so much, "You did alright." When I go up onto that stage, in front of all those people, I carry a photo of you in my pocket. I know you're not really there, but it gives me a sense of your strength, and it helps me feel brave enough to do it.

David, your death has been an overwhelmingly negative experience. I would do anything to have you back. For me, for Mum and Dad, for the rest of our family, and for your friends. And most importantly, for you, for all you have missed out on. We all miss you immensely and it has been so sad to watch everyone grieve for you.

But I'm not dead. I'm still here. I hope to have a long life ahead of me, and I may as well make it as positive as possible. In fact, I am starting to see that I *deserve* a happy life. You helped me to see that while you were here, and it is still true now that you're gone.

David, since you died I have completed a BSc in Animal Behaviour & Welfare and started a new job at an animal shelter. I get to cuddle kittens, and I go to schools and teach children about animal care. I actually get paid to do something that I enjoy so much. You would be so happy for me. And because of the strength you taught me, *I* am happy for me, too.

It has been six years since you died, and I believe I will always miss you. But you taught me many important lessons about valuing myself, which will never die. A part of you is always with me and has become part of me. I will try to live the best, happiest life possible, for you, and all you have missed out on. But I will not do it your way; I will do it mine. Because you taught me that I have to do what works for me, not other people, not even you.

David, I believe that if you could see me now, you would be very proud. That makes me very happy, and sad, but mostly happy.

Laura Williams

Adam and me (Rebekah)

$\mathscr{I}$ thought June 2, 2016 was going to be a normal day.

Since it was the last day of school, my plan was to go to work, say good bye to my students and then start my summer vacation at the end of the day. During the close of homeroom (7:45ish), I got a group text from my brother, Adam, to my mom, my dad and me. I opened it and the text read, "I am sorry. This is not your fault. I love you guys."

Having gone through depression and having suicidal thoughts myself and knowing my brother was on his path to recovery, I knew the meaning of this text. I immediately texted my mom and told her that something was wrong. She replied that she was on it. Time seemed to drag on and on. While I was waiting for a text or some kind of answer from my family, class was still going on, so I had to put on a brave face and push through. Going through my head was that my brother had overdosed on either drugs or prescription pills since he was known to take them.

It was now 2nd period (9:00 AM) and there was no answer from my family. I called my mom. It rang and rang and went to voicemail. I called my dad, he answered, and I asked him what was going on. He answered that Adam was still breathing and they were heading to the hospital. I immediately hung up, got my teacher partner to watch my class and ran to the front to let my principal know what was going on. I saw him in the cafeteria and practically fell into his arms with tears running down my face, sobbing. He was already aware of the situation before I was since my husband contacted him to let him know he was on his way to get me.

Fast forward: we finally get to the hospital downtown, go through the emergency room doors and my husband tells the security guard that we were there for my brother with a gunshot wound to the head. Remember, I still thought my brother had overdosed on drugs so in my mind, I thought the doctors would pump his stomach, and we would get him into a rehab facility and then have him move home. When I heard that he shot himself in the head, I collapsed to the floor in a ball, sobbing.

After that, everything from that day is a blur. I remember some things here and there. The thing that I remember the most was the constant urge to throw up and the anticipation of wondering if he was going to survive.

By the end of the day, my brother was in critical but stable condition. At that point, he was in a medically induced coma so that he could try to heal. My brother spent the next two months in the hospital. We would have "good" days where my brother would be stable and then bad days where he would need surgery, or a tracheotomy added or would have pneumonia and some kind of infection that he would be constantly battling.

I have spent the past two months visiting my brother in the hospital. He didn't look like the same 23-year-old brother that I knew.

His glow was gone; he lay there, lifeless with a machine forcing him to breathe. The date was August 6, 2017.

The night before, I had a break down and cried myself to sleep about my brother. I was his older sister; I was supposed to protect him. My husband told me that he was going to take me to visit my brother. I didn't want to. I didn't want to see him just lay there.

In my eyes, that was not my brother. Even though I fought my husband on it, we ended up going to the hospital. I walked into the hospital room and I saw my brother laying there with a tissue up his nose. I thought he had a nosebleed, but my parents explained to me that his brain was leaking fluid. At that point, the doctor told them there was nothing else they could do and that this would most likely be the state my brother would be in if we kept him alive.

My parents decided to make the tough decision to take my brother off life-support that night.

My world stopped. I was going to become an only child. August 8th, 2017, my brother finally passed and went to be with Jesus.

The first year without him was the hardest. There were days where I wanted to go be with him, but I had to stay strong for my husband and my daughter.

Starting year two has been a little better, but there are still days where my heart aches for him, and I just want to see him one more time. To give him one more hug. There are still questions that go unanswered as to why he would do this, but I can only speculate. I love him, and I know that one day I will see him again in Heaven.

I never thought my brother would commit suicide. Neither did anyone else. He was always the one that welcomed people, the one that was very social. Suicide is a mental disease that can affect anyone. If you or someone you know has urges of self-harm, please seek help. 1-800-273-8255

Rebekah Jernberg

My brother, Bobby

*T*he last time I saw my brother Bobby was Dec 26, 2016. He was 23 years old and looked like he was in his element working at the local, ice skating rink sharpening skates. I remember watching him working and feeling so happy as he was smiling and handing out skates. He finally found a job in a field he loves, hockey.

My brother's dream was to play hockey. He joined a learn-to-skate program the year prior, and shortly joined a team called the *Benders.*

People at the rink loved him so much that they offered him a job.

After Christmas, the last thing my brother wanted to do was skate with me before I headed back to my home in Seattle. Unfortunately, he got called into work, so my Mom and I decided if we couldn't go skating with him, then we would visit him at work and take a few laps around the rink. We decided to get some Mexican food after Bobby was done with his shift. While at the restaurant, the waitress asked if he wanted a margarita. Bobby, who never turned down a recommendation, agreed to his very first margarita. I'll never forget his brain freeze face and the response after, "I will never get this frozen again!"

My mom and I were dying laughing. After dinner, Bobby got called back into work for a closing issue and, just like that, we hugged and said good bye. I still cry when I think back to that last time I saw him.

I always knew Bobby was more likely to die before me. I was seven years old when my younger sister Chrissy and I watched my Mom crying in the hospital room. Her new born baby was stripped from her and sent to Boston Children's Hospital for immediate surgery.

Bobby was diagnosed with hypoplastic left heart syndrome. In laymen's terms, he had half a heart and a 50% chance of surviving the surgery. Bobby survived that day and two more surgeries by the age of three. No one knew how long Bobby would live.

It was a taboo subject that Bobby would always find a way to make us laugh about it.

After so many open-heart surgeries, Bobby had a large scar down his chest to which he told people it was a shark bite or was the result of a knife fight.

Bobby had a heart attack Dec 24, 2015, to which he survived. That last year of his life he lived to the fullest in every way possible. He passed away February 2, 2016 from another heart attack.

Bobby was a beautiful soul who found the beauty in the smallest things life had to offer. Every day with him was a gift that I will never forget.

Thank you, Bobby, I miss you, kid.

This is a song I wrote for you, Bobby, called, "The best the world could ever give."

I'm jealous of the wind
That ripples through your wings
Heart so pure and braver than I knew
Wish it was me and not you

Silence in the room
But love in the air
One look at you and I just knew
I'd never hear your laugh again

I wished you had the best the world could ever give
I told you when I met you I'd protect you till the end
But I always thought we had more time to grow out our innocence

It's hard for me to say
Now that you're away
I'll be happy without you

It feels guilty to love
With a hole in my heart
One look at you and I just knew
I'd never hear your laugh again

Holding back the tears
Stay strong for my Mom
Heart so pure and braver than I knew
Why not me before you

I wished you had the best the world could ever give
I told you when you left me that there's nothing to forgive
I always thought we had more time to grow out our innocence
It's hard for me to say
Now that you're away
I'll be happy without you

Love,

Gia

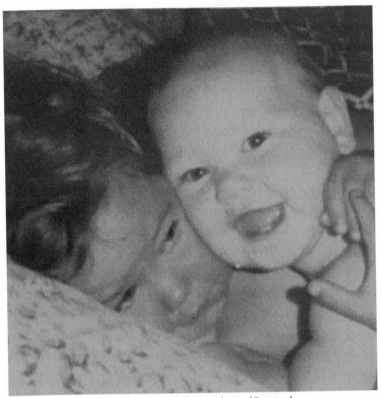

My sister, Danielle, and me (Devon)

Her love was unlike anything I have ever experienced. Solid; unwavering, and always met with patience and understanding. I, on the other hand, can't be described as such.

I've allowed life's injustices to harden me. I always wore a suit of armor, trying so desperately to protect my heart from pain. She was the yang to my yin. She was my sister, born September 9th, 1982, almost exactly 2 years younger, as I had been born September 12th, 1980.

I don't remember the days before she was born. I do, however, vividly remember a night when I was around 8, she 6, where I lay in bed, having to go pee, trying to hold it as long as possible, before I finally woke Danielle, so she could escort me to the only bathroom we had downstairs.

Even though I was older, I was afraid to go downstairs by myself, Danielle was not. I nearly started peeing before I even sat down and, before I could realize that the toilet seat lid was down, I peed on it and all over the floor. We laughed so hard.

Danielle loved all creatures, big and small. She'd occasionally torture me by chasing after me with a snake or a spider. She'd be in a dress outside, digging in dirt to find her next creepy-crawly pet. I was in jeans and a t-shirt, wanting absolutely nothing to do with dirt or creepy-crawlies.

I remember the time, someone in high school came up to me and said so-in-so tried to talk crap about you in our home economics class, and your sister overheard it and shut it down really quick. Or that time a girl showed up in the parking lot after school, Danielle, knowing we had some ridiculous drama and she was always wanting to fight me, saw her car pulling up. She threw her backpack and books on the ground and came flying across the parking lot, looking tough, immediately asking "What's going on?" as if her 5'7 110 lb. frame was going to wreck anyone that dared to screw with me. She would have, though, and I know it, not because she had a problem with the girl, but because she had a problem with anyone who messed with someone she loved.

You see, while Danielle was the patient, kind, unfaltering lovely person, she also appeared to be the one someone could easily destroy. While, I, the angry, pessimistic, mouthy one, appeared to be the one people would fear. I liked it that way, it was easier to keep people at arm's length, not close enough to see my faults; far enough away that I could protect my heart from the inevitable pain that caring and loving someone brings to you.

Danielle was strength; she didn't fear anything, not even loving me.

There were times growing up that I was so cruel to her. She didn't deserve it, she never did, but I bullied her because I could, because she was there, and I was angry for so many reasons, but didn't have the tools at the time to verbalize it. Yet, she kept loving me. Despite all my faults, shortcomings, and just plain shitty behavior, she loved me. She really knew me and still loved me, consistently and without fail.

For the rest of my days here on this earth, I will feel broken. There may always be a sadness that surrounds me. Not just for my loss, but for the loss Danielle's children are feeling, the loss my parents are experiencing, and for all the moments Danielle will not be present here on earth to witness. All the times she won't be here to hold her children when they have joyful, exciting moments, or the moments where they're experiencing pain and they want their mom to hold and love them through it. For the moments my daughter really could use an auntie, but no longer has one, and doesn't know what it feels like to have one.

Devon Belanger

Meghan & Erin

$\mathcal{I}$ don't think that I remember the very last time that I saw you, Erin. It was probably very early in the morning when I looked in on you while you were sleeping before I went off to work. I was excited because I had taken the whole next day off for a dentist appointment, figuring we could hang out before and after. I remember our text conversation throughout the day about the chaos of your work schedule and, when I didn't hear back from you in the afternoon, I never imagined that you were gone.

I remember all the fun that we had throughout our lives, making up dances to our favorite TRL videos, making sheet forts and spending all day in the blankets, walking our dog through the woods, and getting ready for dances. I laugh when I think of how we never actually used each other's names. Instead, choosing from one of a million matching nick names we had. I love the memories of all our art projects and random experiments. I think of when you used to drive me to high school and you hated it as much as I loved it.

I think of your smile every time I see a bright sunflower and remember how much you loved them. I miss you when I go shopping for clothes, wishing to hear you decisively tell me what would look good and what to put back right away. I often want to call you when I'm driving to mindlessly talk about anything and everything. To hear you ask, "Where you be?" and expect an exact answer even though I never quite know where I am. When I feel myself being awkward sometimes I can almost hear you playfully teasing me. A million times every day I think of all the times you jokingly asked, "What would you do without me?" Usually after you filled in one of my sparse memories; like when I asked if you remembered the "Playground on top of that hill" and you knew exactly what I meant.

I think about our struggles with mental health and addiction. Every time I hear open conversations about these topics and progress being made in these areas, I feel joy for the people facing these issues, and then I feel sadness that you are not here to be a part of the movement forward. Every moment of joy in my life is over shadowed by sadness that you are not there, that I cannot include you or talk to you.

I've looked up to you every day, minute, and second of my life; to the point where it drove you crazy at times. You are never truly gone because I still look up to you and think of you every step of my way. I try to make better, more considerate, more daring choices. I try to live in a way that carries meaning, in a way that you will make you proud.

When I think about all of this I cry for myself, I cry for our parents, I cry for our pets that you loved so much, and for your friends whose lives you impacted; but most of all I cry for you. For everything you were, everything you could have been, your clever arguments, timely humor, and the change you could have created in the world. I cry for the amazing person you were and what the world is missing without you.

At the same time, I'm so thankful that I got to share the first part of my life with you. You were all in, in everything you did and you radiated confidence and conviction. I'm lucky to be your sister and I'm proud of everything about you.

I guess to answer your question, I don't know what I'm doing without you. Every step further that I take feels wrong without you here. I guess that without you here I will strive to be more like you because the world needs more people like you in it.

Love you, soul sister,

Meghan

Me (Liz) and my brother, Lou Costanzo

$\mathcal{M}$y last memory of you was on October 25th, 2014. It was the day you took your last breath.

I held your hand, told you that we were all here. *Both grammas are waiting for you. It's okay, you can let go. We will be okay.* As I held your hand and said those words I watched and felt you take one last breath, and then you left this world.

In that moment, a part of me died. Life never prepared me to live without you, without my other half.

We always planned to grow old together. We were 364 days apart. You were, and always will be, a part of my soul, my other half. I was so angry at you. For the first time in our lives, it seemed in that moment, you took my advice and left this world.

We were inseparable our whole lives, and now I was lost and paralyzed by the depth of a pain I never knew existed. Nothing in life ever prepares you. *Nothing.* Losing a sibling is an emptiness that no words can ever describe.

My second worst memory of you was your one-year angelversary day. It was the second hardest day of my life. I felt cornered, having to face the fact that you have been gone a whole year already. I came home and cried to the point I couldn't breathe.

I still don't know how to stop the pain or how to catch my breath sometimes.

It was in that moment of despair, I reached for a bottle of pills, feeling I couldn't go on without you any longer. I began to swallow them, crying and pleading with you, with God. Not knowing how to live with this day after day, night after night. It was in that moment, my life changed forever.

I felt a presence deep within my soul. It was bigger than anything I ever felt in my life. It was so strong, I froze. I heard your voice and saw your face, telling me to stop.

Just stop.

I heard you over and over again, repeating those words. It was almost a type of scared straight moment in my life. I stopped taking the pills and dropped to the floor crying, uncontrollably. You promised to help me through. In return, I promised to help anyone along this horrific journey. I will never forget that day nor the presence in that moment. It was the last day, I ever had a grief attack. You were always my mentor. What I am coming to learn is even in your death, you are my greatest teacher and mentor. You are teaching me so much about death, about life, about the human soul. It was in that moment, I decided to find you again.

I refused to accept you were gone from my life. Through the mists of the pain, you are teaching me that the very essence of life itself is truly amazing and beautiful. Your vibrant spirit lives on, not only inside my heart, but in everything I do, and everywhere I go. You are still my guiding life force. It may not be the way that I want or like. I will always miss your physical presence and wish you were here with me.

So, I began to go on a quest to find you. I came to realize that if I knew everything about you when you were alive, it only made sense for me to follow you on your death journey. I refused to let you go. You gently took my hand and guided me on my spiritual quest. I began to read and learn everything I could about God, Heaven, afterlife, and signs. What I'm finding, and learning is to look deeper into the very essence of life in itself as well as our existence of the eternal soul.

Love is the bridge that connects us.

The power of the human spirit, our true nature of being. Coming to understand, there's no death or separation. There's only a change in worlds into the heavenly realm. There's only a thin veil that separates us. You're still here, ever present in my life—just in a different way. I may not like this new way. I will forever miss your physical presence. However, I am coming to accept that you're, in a sense, teaching me a new language.

A new way of communicating.

You are the light through the darkness, guiding and helping me along.

My greatest memory of you today is when I close my eyes, learning to cross through the veil. I see glimpses of you again. I can hear you, I can feel you.

I found you.

God promises to carry us through the darkness and to lead us into the light. *I got it*. By God, I understand the true meaning of this.

Thank you, God, for showing me the way and carrying me out of the darkness and into the light. For not forsaking me in my time of need and freeing me from the bondage from within. The light is learning to rise above the earthly circumstances in life and to allow the power of the human spirit to be our guide. To awaken to our own true divinity within ourselves. To open up to this life force, the power of the spirit. When we come to learn there is no death; there is no separation, our loved ones transition onto another level of life, the heaven world, and they return to who they truly were.

As we enter the school of life, we learn to awaken our soul—the very nature of our existence. When we finally learn that we are all connected by this invisible force, we are one. That's when we can truly begin to awaken to this truth.

This is without a doubt, the hardest lesson we will ever endure. I know the depth of pain along this journey. Above all, wanting to leave. But I made a promise to my brother to help anyone I can through this. Today, I help run a physical support group as well as an online support called "Loss of a Sibling, healing journey" and the other group is called "God's Healing Spirit after Loss" which is more spiritual based.

If my story touches one life, then I know I honored and kept my promise to my brother and to God. Go on your own journey and explore, you will find that your loved ones are still present in your life, only in a different way. We have free choice to learn or we can close the heart off and never let them in.

It's in the death of the soul that we are reborn again.

Search, seek and look deeper into the very essence of life in itself. You will come to learn, know and feel our loved ones walk beside us, guiding and helping us every step of the way. They will always be our guiding light through the darkness. It's learning to return to the love in our hearts. Learning to hold onto the love to help carry us through.

Love is the bridge that connects us. It's all about learning to connect the dots, to step back and understand what they are trying to teach us about, life, death, God, and eternity. The power of their spirit lives on. We are all connected by this invisible life force.

We are one.

Elizabeth Costanzo Goley

Kristina Ulmer, Katie Amodei

Katie Amodei, age 29, died in a car accident on October 12, 2014. She was my only sibling.

Messages for my sister

By Kristina Ulmer

Day one | October 13, 2014

What can I say to you? You are so far away now, yet I feel you so close. I'm angry at you. For leaving me here all alone. There is a hole in me, that special place only reserved for sisters.

You were so excited when I found out I was having another girl. "Just like us," you said. And I had already thought the same thing. I felt good that Aubrey would have the privilege of being a big sister to a little sister. I knew how special of a job that was. I understood when Jo March said, "I could never love anyone as I love my sisters." It spoke my truth. I was so glad you were able to witness that little life coming out of me, to feel that miracle.

I remember when you were really little, Aubrey's age, me - five, our beds were pushed together because we couldn't sleep apart. You would always fall asleep before me, of course. And you'd be sleeping so deeply, I was sure you had stopped breathing. I would check, my tiny fingers under your nostrils, and I would breathe a sigh as I felt warm air.

One night, years later, those twin beds transformed into a bunk bed, I had the worst nightmare. You had fallen down an elevator shaft and your spirit had come to me for help. No one would listen to me. I couldn't rescue you. You were dying there. I woke up with a start. You were safe, right under me, warmth out of that nose again. Another sigh, but with a pit in my young stomach for days - the dream so vivid.

There were other times too - when you were 19 and away at college... when you collapsed at work that one time... I said prayers and prayers and prayers. I needed to feel that warm breath under your nose again. And then, I did.

A big sister is supposed to protect her little sister. That's the way it works. And I failed you. I'm sorry. I'm so, so sorry. You were a literal piece of me. A piece that is now part of the earth again, the way you'd want it to be. I'm sorry for being selfish and wanting to keep it so much longer.

I love you, my little sister. I love you. I know all those arms enveloped you and swooped you quickly away from this place where you never felt like you quite fit anyway. But you forever left some angel dust behind. Maybe one day, many years from now, I'll use it as breadcrumbs to find my way back home to you.

Rest in peace, my dear, beautiful, one-of-a-kind sister. I will always love you.

Day two-hundred and sixty-six | October 13, 2015

I've learned a lot about tragic and unexpected loss this past year. I've met too many parents who have lost children, too many brothers and sisters who, like me, lost an immense part of their past, present and future in one fell swoop, becoming something that exists in-between an only child and a sibling. We all share in this loss, this knowledge that life is a fleeting and precious gift that can be abruptly ended in the middle of a sentence.

I've learned how large of a shadow can be cast behind. How immense a hole in your heart can be without it causing the muscle to stop beating. How tears can be dry at the saddest moments and flow uncontrollably at the funniest. I have a new regard for true friendship, a deeper love of family, and a new understanding of the profoundness of humanity.

But mostly, I've learned to value every moment provided to me: every laugh of my children, every memory shared between loved ones, every smile from a stranger.

Oh, how I miss you, dear sister. How terribly I miss you. It feels like ages and yesterday all at once that you were here, but I imagine it will always feel this way. I will forever be your big sister and will continue to live my moments for two sets of eyes. I hope that you can see how dear you were to all of us and how much we long for you while we try to appreciate and live joyfully in each new memory without you.

Love you forever.

Day seven hundred and sixty-three | November 13, 2016

This has been a difficult week for many.

Some lost an election and felt like, after finally being heard, they were punched in the gut, knocking the wind out of them so that they temporarily couldn't recover their newly found voices. Some won an election, but were viciously attacked, losing relationships with those they thought knew their hearts. Others, well, most others, were so disgusted by either choice they chose to abstain from the process completely, sticking their heads in the sand.

One would think we all lost this week.

But we didn't.

We're here. We're still standing, albeit a little shaken, a little bruised. But *still alive.*

We've learned that we need to be better listeners. We need to care for one another a little more. And most importantly, we need to love a little more.

Today would've been my sister's 32nd birthday. It's still strange to me that she will never reach 30, forever a girl stuck in the last month of her 20's, never marrying, never having children, never feeling like she found her spot to fit in to this world. But boy did she have enough love for three lifetimes.

She loved animals so much that she refused to consume or use any product that harmed them. She was the kid who beat up bullies and defended the belittled and forgotten. She felt desperate about the needy, handing out boxes of food at our local food bank. She loved helping people so much that, in the last months of her life, she dedicated all her free time to becoming an EMT, the goal she was most proud of succeeding. She loved fairness, justice, and equality.

And she loved her friends. She was everyone's best friend because she was loyal and caring and put effort into her friendships.

But most of all, yes, definitely most of all, she loved her family. She loved all of us so much that I wish she had saved just a little of that love for herself, so she too could have felt how incredible her love was.

Kate, it's been two years, one month, and one day since I last talked to you. And our conversation was one that exuded love, you laughing at something Aubrey had done. Even through a text message, just hours before your death, I could feel the love you had for my children.

I see you in my girls every day. When they're bickering and beating each other up. When they're supposed to be going to sleep and one is singing, while the other one is yelling, "Mommy, tell her to be quiet!" When they're hugging each other or performing a song together. And when they're cracking each other up or both daring to do things together they know mommy wouldn't like.

You live in them. And you still love through them. That is clear to me. And I am amazed watching it every day.

Love this life we've been given. We only have one. And love always. Life is too short for anything else.

That is our purpose.

P.S. Thanks for helping me find that card with your handwriting so I could get that tattoo you always begged me to get. You lied. It hurt. But it was worth it.

Day eight hundred and twenty-six | January 15, 2017

Dear Kate,

This morning I was putting away Christmas decorations, and I was listening to the girls in the other room play whatever weird game they had concocted up. And I wished you were here for me to send this picture to. I'd tell you how happy I am that Ellie is finally at an age that she and Aubrey can now play together, with no adult involvement. You'd say how awesome that is and how the picture reminds you of us at those ages, playing in the wee hours of the morning in our bedroom while our parents slept down the hall, which is exactly the reason why I would've sent you the picture in the first place. And then we'd exchange some inside jokes, ones only two people who shared a siblinghood and, more specifically, a sisterhood together could swap.

It's been two years, three months, and four days since I last talked to you. And there hasn't been one of those 826 days that I haven't thought about you.

There are days where you're there in a memory: your goofy grin while singing *Newsies* or *Les Mis*; your proud smile while holding Ellie after watching her birth; your determined brow while debating some topic you were passionate about; your eyes rolling when I tried to teach you some important life lesson big sisters try to impart on their little sisters. These moments, while bittersweet, make me smile and remind me that you are always there in me, even if you're not with me.

And then there are days, moments like right now, that you're not here, not here at all - just out of reach - and I desperately wish to be able to grab your sleeve and yank you back into existence. And then we'd cry and laugh in that way only two sisters can cry and laugh together and talk about how ridiculous and insane this all was. And these are the moments that overwhelm my senses, forcing tears to my cheeks and heaves in my chest.

We don't speak about grief enough as a society. I suppose it's because it's messy and crooked and tangled and unfixable. There's no solution. No political act or magician's trick that can make it vanish through a hat. Once it strikes, it sits there, on your heart, becoming an inoperable tumor. It never shrinks as some suggest "time heals all wounds." But you learn to live with it, the way one adapts to living with a missing limb. You will have happiness, a lot of happiness if you allow yourself to.

It'll just be a little lopsided.

Until again,

Your sister

Day one thousand and ninety-eight | October 14, 2017

It's been three years and two days since I last talked to you. And for each new moment there has been without you, there have been just as many moments I have thought about you.

But keeping you alive through memories is not the same as you being alive. It doesn't even suffice.

Tonight, I spent bedtime storytime telling tales about us as children. How we'd pretend the ceiling of our Hulmeville bedroom was covered with food. You'd gobble up a slice of cake, plucked from the heavens of the dull white drywall. Me, some ice cream, a pear, a strawberry or two. We'd stuff ourselves full of our imaginations until our giggles rang too loud and Mom would come in to scold us for not sleeping.

I told them how we'd push our beds together. How we'd pretend the crack was a dark abyss and we'd "save" each other from being eaten by it. I told them how you woke up early one morning, no more than Ellie's age, and watched a frightening PG-13 movie, instilling that you would forever fear our deep, dark closet, yet while sparking your heartthrob flame for Stephen Dorff.

I told Thanksgiving stories, Christmas stories, and Halloween stories. Anything I could think of as they continued asking for more, thirsty to hear and learn just one more bit about their mommy and her kid sister as children, laughing at each off the wall recollection.

And then, as I snuggled in bed with them, listening to their breathing become heavy with sleep, I thought about Sylvester Stallone's quote from *This is Us* the other night, a show I'm still not sure you'd love or poke fun at me for loving. "In my experience, Kevin, there's no such thing as 'a long time ago,'" Sly says when reminiscing about his children in their youth, implying that Kevin's deceased father is always just in reach because, of course, we can always fondly bring forth our late loved ones in memory.

But the thing is, while poetic, it wasn't exactly true.

It's been three years and two days since I last talked to you. 1,098 days. 26,356 hours. 1,581,375 minutes. However, I count it, it's "a long time ago" and it's too long to have not seen you or spoken with you. And the truth is, as time passes, as every new memory is made, it makes it even longer that any new memories were made with you.

Keeping you alive through memories is not the same as you being alive. It doesn't even suffice. But it's what we have. And so I suppose it will have to do.

And so, I'll keep telling your story, dear sister. You'll live through our voices, through our memories, through my children. And I'll hear you, forever, in each of their giggles, remaining steadfast that however "long time ago" it was, you were here, and you will never be forgotten.

Kristina Ulmer

Rickey Dustin Gibson
Aug. 16, 1979- July 13, 2016

My brother, Rick, and his daughter, Kira Morgan Gibson

Dearest Rick,

I thought the day we lost Dad would be the hardest day we would ever have to go through, but I was wrong.

I still remember how we felt as children. You were my and Ryan's big brother, our hero, our confidant, our best friend—a piece of the puzzle that will now forever be gone, unfinished, forever incomplete...

The last time I saw you is on a constant repeat in my mind. If I had just stayed five minutes longer... If I had just recognized that this time was different. If I could have saved you. If I told you one last time that I loved you... If you knew somehow this was going to be the last time we saw each other. All of these ifs, and I'll never know the answers to them.

I feel so broken and empty without you. It feels like this huge piece of me has literally been seared off of my flesh, and there's nothing that can be done to ever fix it. I keep waiting on the day that I'll feel even remotely normal, but I've finally realized that THAT girl, yeah, she died along with you.

That version of me is forever gone, and I will never get her back, and you know what?

I'm glad.

To have her back now would mean that our love was conditional. That our bond wasn't strong enough. That our love didn't run as deep as it did, and *still* does.

Having that innocent version of me back would diminish the unforgettable, untouchable, impact you made, and continue to make on my life forever.

Ryan, Rick, and me (Nikki)

I will always remember your laugh, your smile, your kindness. I will remember how full of love your heart was. What an amazing son, brother, uncle and, most of all, father that you were.

Thank you for trusting me with your amazing babies! Every time I look at them, I see pieces of you.

You made a mark on this world, and I will remind your children of that every single day until I take my last breath and we are together once again.

I miss you, and long to be with you more than anything. I will always love you to the moon and back, big brother!

Your one and only sister,

Nikki

Broken to Pieces

I'm empty, I'm lost.
I'm scared, I'm broken.
I'm torn, I'm shattered.
I'm ripped, I'm bruised.
Left beaten, bleeding.
All alone to die.
Trying to pick up the pieces,
Pieces that are falling,
Rotting, pieces I'm cutting off.
I sigh, I cry, I rip out my heart.
I hold it, I feel it, there is no pulse.
I hit it, I beat it, the life's draining out.
I'm empty, no beating, no love for the lost.
No life for the broken, my voice isn't heard.
My life's become empty, my soul has been torn.
What's left for me now? No part left unbroken.
Left shattered, left scared, one life left unspoken….

My brother, Brian

*H*ey, Bri,

I just wanted to let you know that I love you so much.

I think of you every waking hour—even in my dreams.

I wish I could say that I'm okay, but the only thing that keeps me going is the thought of me living life for the both of us. I promise that I will work hard to experience and love as much as I can.

I really hope you know how much I love you.

Aaron Soliz

Me (Alvina Garner) and my brother, Darren Privett

$\mathcal{M}$y brother and I had finally gotten close.

He was my only full-blooded sibling. We would tell each other often how much we loved each other, and we talked often.

On March 19th, 2016, we lost our mom, and it was hard. Then, two weeks to the day, on April 2, 2016, my brother was in a car wreck while working his paper route with his son, my nephew, in his sports car.

They jumped a hill that they'd done plenty of times before, but this time, Darren lost control of the car. He wasn't wearing a seatbelt and was ejected from the car.

My brother was killed instantly.

I thank God that he didn't suffer.

My nephew was knocked pretty hard. He suffered road rash and had a dislocated elbow. He lost his Dad.

Luckily, we still had him.

Part of me died on April 2. There's not a day that Darren doesn't run through my mind—the looks he would give me for saying something silly, the little things...

I miss him every day.

Alvina Garner

My brother, Reed Hartner

$\mathscr{O}$ne year and two months have passed, and the thought of you being gone still takes my breath away every time I wake up.

I miss you so much, Reed.

Our last words were cruel. I'm not going to let that define us, though.

We loved as hard as we fought, for you are truly the only person in this world that took my bullshit and loved me anyway.

Oh, how I wish I wasn't writing this.

Only God knows the pain I'm suffering here on earth. It's not the same, nor will it ever be. You are so missed. I don't think you knew how much you were loved.

Mom misses you so much. Dad stays angry at the jails, the court house and the judges.

Whitney Hartner (Reed's wife), Reed, our mom, Sandra Hartner, and me, Heather Waters

I lay around in your hoodies, I smell your dirty laundry.

I wish I could turn back time. If I could, I'd go back and save you somehow.

I miss your hugs. I miss your smile.

Reed and me (Heather)

Drug addiction didn't define you. I want people to know you were not just some junkie off the street that overdosed you were a son, a brother, a husband, a father, an uncle, a nephew, and a friend.

You would give the shirt off your back to the homeless man down the street. You would hold your niece all night while she cried as she was teething because I couldn't.

Your death has rocked my world. I cry more now than I have ever cried in my life. My grief seems to worsen as the time goes by.

I'm in therapy now to help control this overwhelming pain that is now my life. It's not like losing a grandparent. It's way worse. I lost a part of ME when you died.

On the night of April 6, 2017, my brother went to Heaven. He snorted heroin for the last time.

I will forever have a broken heart.
Forever35
I love you, Reed Hartner

Love your sissy,
Heather

$\mathcal{M}$y sister, Bethany Meagan, was born on January 31, 1998. I was 14 years old. I remember seeing her that day and being so happy and so very proud to be a big sister for the second time.

My other sister, Amanda, and I would go to our Dad and bonus mom's (I say "bonus mom' because she is so much more than a step-mom) every other weekend and holidays, and part of summer. We were in awe of her every time we were there and saw her.

Bethany was always changing between the times we were there. I remember one time we were eating chicken nuggets. I don't remember from what restaurant, but she had a fast food cup and her chicken and a pile of ketchup. She was sticking the straw in the ketchup and then licking it then she would dip back in the ketchup and then again in her cup.

She LOVED ketchup.

She loved eating spaghetti noodles with only parmesan cheese, no sauce or meat.

She was so special in every way. She loved to dance since she was a little bitty and was a wonderful dancer. We went to every dance recital the first weekend of June. I looked forward to that first weekend in June every year. I got to see my baby sister dance.

I always called her my baby sister.

She had her own fist bump. My dad would hold his fist out, and she would hit it with the palm of her hand. He would pick on her and she, and everyone else, would just laugh.

In 2016, I got to go to their house several times. They live about 2 hours away so we (my kids and myself) don't get to go a whole lot. In May of 2016, I watched my baby sister walk across the stage and earn her high school diploma. She graduated with honors and probably with the most scholarships. But she wouldn't turn them all in. She said it wasn't their business. She just didn't want everyone knowing how smart she really was.

Beth and I (Wendy) at graduation.

She knew a lot of different languages. She loved French! Beth had letters from almost every state in the United States. That summer she changed her name to Lucinda Kay Luna. She had her mind made up for years, and that summer, she changed it. She told everyone that she would be Luci or Beth. She didn't care which one people wanted to call her.

We went back a few weeks later, the first weekend of June, for her last dance recital. She was 18 years old and had just graduated. That year, I told her that I was still coming to their house the first weekend in June because it was a tradition every year to go up that weekend.

Beth's Dance Recital

We went back at Labor Day, Thanksgiving, and Christmas.

A few days after Thanksgiving, we were having to leave, and she was going to work. My oldest daughter asked to wake her up, so she could tell her aunt bye. I took a picture of them together—

one that I will always treasure. At Christmas, we were back for a few days. One day, my bonus mom was going to McDonalds. Some of my kids were going to ride with her and so was Luci. I suddenly had this feeling to go with them, so it ended up being just my bonus mom, sister, and me that went.

Well she got in the front seat and I sat behind her. On the way, I reached up and pulled her hair. She hollered, "Mom she's touching me!" Then I touched her neck. She hollered, "Mom she's in my bubble!" I didn't think she was going to able to drive home she was laughing so hard at us. She said she hasn't heard that in so many years. When she did hear it was always because Beth was bugging our other sister and me.

In saying all this, sadly, 2016 was the lasts. The Last Time I Saw You.... The last dance recital, last Thanksgiving, last Christmas, the last picture I ever took of her was of her and my daughter at Thanksgiving, and the last Christmas with her. I did talk and text with her in 2017, but my main last memories of spending time with her was in 2016.

On June 1, 2017, my sister was accidentally shot. I don't want to go through all the details of that. No one went to jail as it was a complete and total accident. I don't blame anyone. The person that did it is very dear to me, and I do forgive this person. I hope they can go on with their life and not let this destroy them.

My sister wouldn't want that at all. She loved this person dearly.

She passed away early in the morning on the 2nd. Later that day, I was at home packing to go to my dad and bonus mom's house, and it hit me that the first weekend of June I was always packing to go for a fun weekend and watch my sister dance. Well,

226

that year, the first weekend of June, I was packing to go tell my sister goodbye. It was so hard trying to pack.

The next few days were difficult: picking out songs for her funeral, being there for family, and trying my hardest to stay strong. Her visitation and funeral were hard, but also a celebration of her life. We smiled a good bit because people were telling their memories. Some didn't like this funeral, but it was what helped my dad and bonus mom. That's what counted, to help them the best that it could. It was a hard-enough day, but hearing memories made it a little easier. Hearing songs that she loved made it a little easier, too.

I didn't see my sister a whole lot. We only saw each other maybe two or three times a year, but she was my baby sister. I was so proud of the woman she was becoming. I'm so glad I told her that a lot. I really believe that she knew how special she was to me. This past year has been so horrible. Facebook has memories, and there's some that make me smile and some that will make me cry. I look every day to see when my sister would comment on something or like something.

I love you so much, Luci! My baby sister you will always be!

This may not help anyone get through losing their sibling because I really don't have the words to help you get through. I am still slowly getting through this myself, and it's very hard. But, you will live—you will make it. I have many days that I cry, and I have some days that I laugh at a memory. Like the memory of "She's in my bubble." I smile and laugh every time I think of that. It's okay to cry, but it's also okay to laugh!

God has been the only one to get our family through this. I don't what your religion is or if you believe in God or not, but for some of my family and for me, God has been the one that has helped more than anyone or anything!

Wendy Morris

$\mathcal{M}$y sister, Lindsey Denee

$\mathcal{F}$or all the people out there, that have lost a sibling, I am very sorry. I can't help you much as I am still just a kid myself.

My sister, Lindsey Denee, had a nickname: Lili. So, we always called her Lili.

Even though I didn't get to meet her, I know she was an amazing big sister, and I love her.

I actually got my name from her.

The day my mom went in for the sonogram and found out I was a girl, Lili said that she wanted to call me Jasmine. She told everyone that I was her "baby sister, Jasmine". When my mom called me Haily, she said, "No, it's my sister, Jasmine. I also have her middle name, Denee. My name is Haily Jasmine Denee.

She passed a month before I was born.
She passed nine days before her fifth birthday.

I heard a lot of things about Lindsey from my mom, like how she would only eat the "Kraft Mac & Cheese" and not the "Velveeta Mac & Cheese".

I Love Lili, and I wish I could grow up with her.

I also had a sister named Kristin.

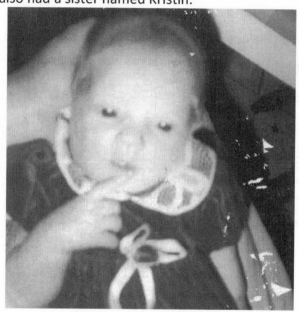

My sister, Kristin

We call her Krisi. I don't know much because she was three months old and was very sick when she passed in 2004. That was 3 years before I was born. I also miss her.

Jasmine Morris

10 years old

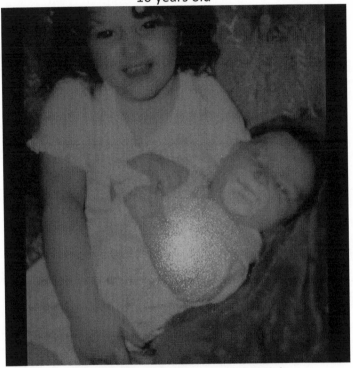

My sister, Lindsey, and me (Emily)

I don't remember a lot about my sister, Lindsey. Some people, like family and my mom's friends, called her Lili.

My cousin Brian (he was just a few months older than her) couldn't say Lindsey, so he called her Lili, so everyone started calling her by that name.

She was about to have her fifth birthday, nine days before she passed. I don't know much of what happened that night except that she was sick. I had stayed with my Aunt Charlotte while my mom and dad took Lili to the hospital.

She passed before I got home the next day.

Her last words were, "How is my sister, Emily?" My mom told her that I was okay and playing. Then Lindsey said, "I love you, Mommy!"

A few hours later she passed away.

That is all I know, and I love her. She would not let anything hurt me. She loved me. I wish I could remember her. I was one year and 8 months old when she passed.

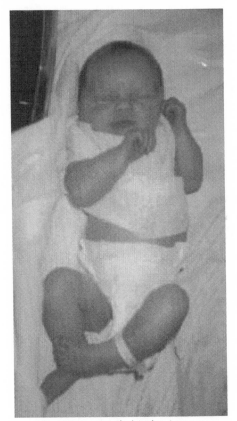

My sister, Krisi's birth picture.

I have another sister, Kristin. We called her Krisi. I don't know a lot about her. She was 3 months old, and I wasn't born until two years after she passed away. I do know that she was very sick from the time she was two weeks old.

I do miss them both.

Emily Morris

12 years old

*N*ow, you can take a breath.

Go ahead and wipe your tears, and try not to be so sad, because you're not alone.

Grief is truly a process.

Be mad, be angry, be sad.

Don't apologize for your emotions.

Figure out your "new normal".

Someone told me after my brother passed that losing a sibling was a lot like getting a broken arm. It hurts, but eventually it heals. It may never be the same, and that's okay.

You'll figure it out.

Just don't give up.

You are loved.

Danielle

Made in the USA
Middletown, DE
03 March 2021

34724555R00139